The Astonished Heart

*Reclaimimg the Good News from the
Lost-and-Found of Church History*

Robert Farrar Capon

William B. Eerdmans Publishing Company
Grand Rapids, Michigan / Cambridge, U.K.

© 1996 Wm. B. Eerdmans Publishing Co.
255 Jefferson Ave. S.E., Grand Rapids, Michigan 49503 /
P.O. Box 163, Cambridge CB3 9BA U.K.

Printed in the United States of America

01 00 99 98 97 96   7 6 5 4 3 2 1

Library of Congress Cataloging-in-Publication Data

Capon, Robert Farrar.
    The astonished heart: reclaiming the good news from the lost-and-found
    of church history / by Robert Farrar Capon.
        p.   cm.
    ISBN 0-8028-0791-7 (pbk.: alk. paper)
    1. Church — Catholicity. 2. Church history. 3. Spiritual life — Christianity.
I. Title.
BT601.3.C36 1995
262'.72 — dc20   95-46080
                                                          CIP

In memory of my grandfather,

Frederick Capon:

the most astonished heart I ever met.

Contents

Acknowledgments

M any friends and colleagues have read the manuscript of *The Astonished Heart* and been gracious enough to give me the benefit of their comments and criticisms. I want to thank, in no particular order,

- Richard Norris, for getting me started on the subject of the forms of the church — especially with regard to the models available to the early church in the Greco-Roman world;
- Larry McCormick, for his help in supplying me with research materials and his observations on and suggestions about the church in the book of Acts;
- Roger Van Harn, for his encouragement as I wrote the book — and especially for the enthusiasm and discernment of his evaluations;
- Loren Mead, for his suggestions about the Exilic period and for his thoughtful criticisms of the draft manuscript, many of which I've responded to in the book;
- Nils Blatz, for catching me nodding on the subject of the "catholicity" of Judaism and for additional reading matter and comments;
- Donald Desmond, for his comments on the manuscript and for his suggestion with respect to the Hebrew Scriptures;
- Robert Wright and Robert Cooper, for suggesting that I try to say something more positive about possible future models of the church; and

ACKNOWLEDGMENTS

- Taylor Stevenson, for persuading me to be less negative about the Christendom model, especially as regards its inevitable role in the church's future.

Last but by no means least, I'm in the deepest of all possible debts to my wife, Valerie. She has typed this book (and most of my others) into the computer, and she has gone over them all with me, aloud and in proofreading sessions, with unflagging attention. She remains my best audience and severest critic: I would never have been able to do what I've done without her. "Strength and honor are her clothing; and she shall rejoice in time to come. Give her the fruit of her hands; and let her own works praise her in the gates."

1. An Overview of
Church History

While this book is indeed about church history, I make no pretense of its being a formal work on the history of the church. It omits too much of what I do know about the subject (not to mention the far greater mass of what I don't know) to deserve any such dignification. Instead, it is a relaxed, and I hope relaxing, ramble through the thirty-five hundred years or so during which that history has been brewing. To put a finer point on it, it's an *argument drawn from church history* designed to demonstrate what I consider to be the egregious mistakes the church has made as the result of turning itself into a *religious institution* and thus losing its grip on its *catholicity.* Whether my argument is convincing will be for you to decide. But since no merely prefatory remarks can help you do that, let me end the prologue right here and get on with the job.

▼   ▼   ▼

For some time now, we've been treated to a good deal of heavy breathing and earnest thumbsucking about the plight of the Christian religion and the problems of the institutional church. The thesis of this book is that almost all of it is wildly off the mark. While it is true that our present dishevelment may well be one of the larger crises (or opportunities) the church has bumped into over its long career, our real difficulty is something else: we have an almost continuous track record of hitting the Christian nail squarely on the thumb. All our noisy hammering to the contrary, the problem is not that we need to get back to the truth of our religion or to get on to some better version of the ecclesiastical institution; rather, it's that we need nothing so much as to stop acting as if we're either a religion or an institution at all.

To begin with, Christianity is not a religion; it's the proclamation of the end of religion. Religion is a human activity dedicated to the job of reconciling God to humanity and humanity to itself. The Gospel, however — the Good News of our Lord and Savior Jesus Christ — is the astonishing announcement that God has done the whole work of reconciliation without a scrap of human assistance. It is the bizarre proclamation that religion is over, period. All the efforts of the human race to straighten up the mess of history by plausible religious devices — all the chicken sacrifices, all the fasts, all the mysticism, all the moral exhortations, all the threats — have been canceled by God for lack of saving interest. More astonishingly still, their purpose has been fulfilled, once for all and free for nothing, by the totally non-religious death and resurrection of a Galilean nobody. Admittedly, Christians may use the *forms* of religion — but only because the church is the sign to the world of God's accomplishment of what religion tried (and failed) to do, not because any of the church's devices can actually get the job done. The church, therefore, must always be on its guard against giving the impression that its rites, ceremonies, and requirements have any religious efficacy in and of themselves. All such things are simply *sacraments* — real presences under particular signs — of the indiscriminate gift of grace that God in Christ has given everybody.

Furthermore, the church that God inspired to be the ongoing sign of such vulgar Good News is not an institution; it is a community of merely human beings entrusted with the proclamation of an astonishingly *catholic* salvation. Institutions are not human. The Congress of the United States, the Presidency, Marriage, the Family, General Motors, IBM — even the Holy See and the First Presbyterian Church of Resume Speed, Indiana — none of these are flesh-and-blood persons. Real people may indeed be members of such ethereal entities; but for all that, the entities themselves are not people for whom Christ died. They are quasi-angelic beings which, in their historical manifestations, are not catholic but *parochial:* by definition, they are always for *some,* never for all. Accordingly, the various institutional forms that the church has historically adopted to accomplish its outrageously all-inclusive proclamation are always incipiently at odds with the catholicity of the Gospel. It is this very catholicity, therefore, that is always the church's most endangered species. To be sure, the church will inevitably, in every period of its history, conform itself to one parochial model or another; but it is essential that it never attach the notion of inevitability to any particular model. As a matter of fact, it will be the burden of this book to show that no model is either directly ordained by God or prescriptively defined in Scripture; rather, every model is selected by the church from *the particular historical context* in which it finds itself at any given point. We do indeed believe that the Holy Spirit provides a certain guidance in this process of selection, but the Spirit neither sanctions the outcomes of the process nor requires that the form selected at one time or place necessarily be the form for all times and places.

This is particularly important to bear in mind in our present context, when most of the forms of the church we've known either have collapsed or are collapsing before our eyes. We are faced, you see, with the task of creating a new form — or even a multiplicity of new forms. It might be nice if we could come up with something a little less dangerous to our catholicity than some of the models we've previously been tempted to try on. But more on that later in the book. Since I shall be spending a good deal of time detailing the dangers of our past forms, let me play my cards face up at this point and give you a highly compressed overview of the mistakes, as I see them, that we've made in the course of our history so far.

The church started out as a movement within Judaism — a movement proclaiming Jesus as both Lord and Messiah. It neither conceived of itself as a new religion nor featured itself as an institution. Had you asked the members of the early Jerusalem church what brand of religion they were practicing, they would have told you, Jewish; had you asked them what institutional structures governed their lives, they would have told you, the Temple and the Synagogue. But by the end of the first century, the church (by then professedly "Christian" and principally located in the Gentile world) had come to see itself quite frankly as both a religion and an institution. To distinguish itself from what it considered the false religions of the Greco-Roman Empire, it was naturally enough tempted to see itself as the *true* religion. But with the hook of religion thus hidden in the bait of truth, the church was caught off guard and quickly became the very thing it should most have opposed: it became, despite its continued profession of catholicity, a merely parochial entity — just one more religion among many. That it was the "right" religion could never make up for the loss of catholicity incurred when it forgot it wasn't a religion at all to begin with.

For no religion can ever be catholic. Every last one, the "Christian religion" included, encompasses not the catholic mass of humanity but only its own particular adherents. The church never has had and never will have — nor in all likelihood was it ever intended to have — every human being in its membership. Moreover, the essence of any religion is its promise that, if it is followed diligently, God will smile on its practitioners. But the Gospel with which the church is entrusted says that God has already smiled on the whole world in Jesus. The *Christian* religion, therefore, is an oxymoron. It is the catholic Good News of the salvation of all turned into the bad news of a parochial proposition about the salvation of some. And much the same thing can be said of the church's acquisition of institutional status. We took a liberated community of believers living in the freedom of unqualified grace and converted it into a navel-watching institution dedicated, inevitably, to the preservation of its own structure. We created a one-eyed monster whose focus would always be on the boring rules it made for yesterday instead of on the astonishing liberty with which Christ had made it free for today. In short, we locked ourselves into the past — and then had the gall to wonder why our present always seemed so dull and our future so terrifying.

This entire disaster took us little more than the first hundred and fifty years of our history to accomplish: the record of it can be read even in the pages of the New Testament. But that was by no means the whole story. Next (after the period of the persecutions, during which our illegality spared us the worst excesses of our status as a religious institution), we became, by the Emperor Constantine's Edict of Toleration, first a *legal* religion and then, very quickly indeed, the *official* religion of the Empire. And with that, a new model of the church was born. We concocted something never before seen on land or sea: we invented the notion of a *Christian society* — in a word, we created *Christendom.* This was by no means all bad. A church proclaiming the incarnation of God in human flesh could fairly be expected to concern itself with all the glories that flesh is heir to, politics included. But once the church had snuggled comfortably into bed with the state, it had an increasingly difficult time avoiding the ills that the flesh is also heir to. Subservience to the state, confusion of the church's ends with the state's ends, competition with the state, and (when the Empire collapsed under the pressure of the barbarians in the West and of Islam in the East) the assumption of the role of the state in the preservation of civil order — all these became problems for us.

Let me move you at warp speed through a thousand years of church history. During the secular anarchy of the Dark Ages and into the flowering of the medieval synthesis in the West, the problems of the institutional structure of the church, while sufficiently manifold to lead to the upheaval of the Reformation, were not overwhelming. But with the rise of nation-states in the fifteenth and sixteenth centuries, the first cracks began to appear in the Christendom model of the church. One of the hard facts of the Reformation was that the only people available to run it were, every last one of them, late medievalists. When they spotted a medieval abuse (for example, the notion that the once-and-for-all saving action of God in Christ could be appropriated only by means of suitably religious works), they quite naturally reformed it with might and main. But when they did not see an abuse for what it was, they just as naturally went right on perpetuating it.

And so it was that when the Reformers came to ask themselves what the relationship of the various reformed churches should be to the several nation-states in which they found themselves, they opted for the old, familiar Christendom model they knew and loved so well: they made *mini-Christendoms* all over Europe. Their reasoning was quite simple: since every baptized person in medieval society had been a member of a single church (in fact, it was precisely by baptism that one became a member of medieval society), every baptized person in the new nation-states would have to be a member of a single church. Everyone in Scotland would have to be Presbyterian; everyone in Saxony, Lutheran; everyone in Bavaria, Roman Catholic; everyone in Geneva, Calvinist; and everyone in England, C. of E. State and church would go right on being one — even at the price of a multiplicity of states and churches.

But this construction of rinky-dink Christendoms was by no means the Reformation's only contribution to the hiding of the astonishment of the Gospel. In spite of the fact that the original Reformers — particularly Luther — began the movement with a liberating rediscovery of free grace and dying love, their successors, assigns, and devisees rapidly obscured that liberty by scholasticizing the stuffing out of it. Every church of the Reformation era (the Roman Church not excepted) fell in love with the idea of confecting long-winded confessions of faith — binding documents that spelled out in mind-numbing detail the correct positions to be held on all points at issue. To list only a few: the Lutherans came up with the Augsburg Confession, the Reformed Churches with the Heidelberg Catechism, the Presbyterians with the Westminster Confession, the Roman Catholics with the Decrees of the Council of Trent and the Creed of Pius the Fifth, and the Church of England (in typically Anglican style) with the giant waffle of the Thirty-nine Articles of Religion.

This was not only a new development but an odd one. The church of the Middle Ages may have won no prizes for keeping the Gospel unobscured, but at least it managed to give the impression that if a candidate for membership could get through to the end of the Apostles' Creed without blinking, he or she had made a sufficient declaration of orthodoxy. Not so in the time of the Reformation.

Every last theological position up for grabs had to be pinned down for subscription by the faithful. But because the various confessional churches were now hand in glove not with a single loosey-goosey secular order but with the several power-hungry nation-states of Europe, it was felt that the faithful could not safely be left free to subscribe to confessions of their individual choice. The ruler of whatever principality they had the bad luck to find themselves in insisted that they sign on the dotted line of his confession. *Cuius regio, eius religio* was the watchword: "Whose the realm, his the religion." The Reformers, by and large, took a dim view of religious liberty; most of them, barring a handful of wild-eyed fringe types, couldn't even conceive of it.

Fast forward now. By one of the coincidences of history, the Reformation occurred at the beginning of the Age of Exploration, and that coincidence gave rise to a pair of consequences that would be devastating to the church. The first was the growth of trade, based largely on the opportunities provided by the discovery of the New World. The second was the settlement of the newly acquired territories — a development which, by the logic of the times, entailed the exportation of the now various versions of Christianity to places that were not yet nation-states.

Consider first the consequences of the burgeoning of mercantile activity. On the Reformation principle that no one in Scotland, say, was supposed to have any truck with people who were not Presbyterians (or no one in Saxony with non-Lutherans, or no one in England with non-Anglicans), you might have thought that the business of buying and selling would have suffered a crimp sufficient to inhibit trade altogether. But that didn't happen. What did happen was that all the traders who couldn't do business with each other on their home turf found themselves someplace where they could. And that someplace was the Low Countries, where the Dutch were enjoying such mercantile success that they thought it a shame to allow religion to come between people who had goods to sell and money to spend. And so it was not only that the notion of religious toleration first saw the light of day in the Netherlands but also that, as the seventeenth and eighteenth centuries progressed, a similar dawning occurred in the realm of philosophy. In England, for example, John Locke rejected the notion of the divine right of kings — and then went bravely on to espouse the doctrine that would eventually blow the assorted Christendoms of the Reformation right out of the water, namely, the political theory that every individual had a right to freedom of property, thought, worship, and speech. And with that, please note, we're only a short fifty years or so away from the Declaration of Independence, the Constitution, and the inalienable rights of (mostly) everybody.

But go back a bit now and consider the second consequence of the Reformation coincidence: the settlement of the New World. The émigrés from Europe who arrived on its shores brought their religions with them. Some, but by no means all, came to escape religious persecution — only, alas, to practice it themselves the first chance they got. The rest, however, simply continued to practice the religion they had in hand wherever they landed, usually in the company of their co-religionists. In either case, the result was that, by accident or design, some areas became predominantly Congregational, or Anglican, or Roman Catholic (in the Massachusetts Bay Colony, the Virginia Colony, and the Baltimore Colony, respectively), while others became religiously diverse as the result of successive waves of immigrants (New Amsterdam/New York). But it was the rule of diversity that finally triumphed. By the time the American colonies were ready to set up shop on their own, sociological pressures coupled with Lockean principles had already made a European-style establishment of any one religion impossible. The Christendom model of the church was suffering from more than just cracks in its foundations and holes in its walls; it was a prime candidate for the wrecker's ball.

And therefore, after some thirteen hundred years of dubious service to the church, Christendom made the penultimate misstep in its long march away from the church's Gospel beginnings. As if it weren't bad enough that the community of the Good News had become first a religion, then a religious institution, then a societal religious institution, then *the* societal religious institution, and then a collection of societal religious institutions, we proceeded to bring forth the anomaly that continues to haunt us to this day: we turned it into a free-for-all of *competing Christian religions.*

I won't belabor the remainder of our history here. Suffice it to say that the Christendom model of the church died a well-deserved death in the early nineteenth century; that it was replaced (especially in America) by the equally inept but less hardy corporate model; that the corporate model is now in almost total collapse; and that we are currently sitting in the rubble of all this history, wondering what in the world will happen to us next. You have my promise that in the rest of this book I shall not only fill you in on the details of these more recent disasters but also try to suggest, if not what our future model will be, then at least what models we are currently being encouraged (or tempted) to buy. From what I've already given you, none of this should come as much of a surprise — because, as I've maintained with every previous model of the church, the only place we can find new forms is the present *historical context in which we live.*

We won't discover them by going back to earlier eras because, God help us, we are people of this era only. And we cannot discover them by guessing our way forward into the future because whatever help God may give, it does not extend to providing us with diagrams of tomorrow's history. My only insistences about the new models, therefore, will be these: first, that they are already lying around somewhere, right under our noses; second, that some of them will turn out to be better (and some, I'm afraid, much worse) than what we have previously latched onto; and third, that to choose between them without repeating the mistakes of our history, we will need to look very closely indeed at what that history has to teach us.

Here ends the preliminary overview. Time now for a short diversion on the perils of the territory that we, as the church, happen to occupy at the present time.

2. *A Look at Where We Are Now*

The various theological positions that we as Christians hold on any subject are usually laid out along the old three-part political spectrum of right, center, and left. For the better part of a century, we've named ourselves (or been branded by others as) conservatives, moderates, or liberals. But because those classifications are now overworn with use, not to mention overcharged with emotional static, I'm going to propose, just for the fun of it, a less value-laden division — one based on *geography* and *atmospheric conditions.* I shall characterize our conservative sisters and brothers as those who find the theological atmosphere at *sea level* most congenial, those who are in the middle as our friends who prefer the more varied climate of *the uplands,* and those at the liberal end of things as compatriots who thrive best in the thin air of *the mountaintops,* if not the stratosphere. Just remember one thing: they're all *us.*

Look first at those of us who breathe the air at sea level. Our habitat here is the terrain where the life of the world meets the vast ocean from which it sprang — where humanity meets God, where the light of reason meets the revelation of Scripture, and where the safety of the bounded meets the fearful yet fascinating mystery of the boundless. It is as good a place as any to live, even if it can be hot and humid in the south and frozen and forbidding in the north. For its inhabitants, however, it has one compelling feature: for those of us here, it is the ocean that defines the place — the ocean to which we give precedence and deference. For us who delight in this place, revelation counts more than reason. If a truth can be found in Scripture, it becomes a truth so paramount that it overrides all other "truths" and puts them in quotation marks to boot.

But here, too, flourish forbidding tribes. Here are those of us who know for certain that homosexuality is an abomination, that lesbianism is wrong, that abortion is nothing but murder, that the atonement is limited, and that God predestines some to hell — all for no other reason than that we have collected those unlovely shells (to the exclusion of more comely ones) from the beaches of Scripture. Our preference here is for rare and grotesque shells — and we can take a shell from one beach and make it a rule for all beaches. Here, in short, we are convinced that the ocean we defer to is a sea of uniform truths, any one of which is no less true in and of itself than is the ocean as a whole.

To our credit, this territory of preference keeps us close to the living water and attentive to its every wave and ripple. At our best here, we receive the ocean's treasures and ponder its depths not because we have managed to reduce its riches to plausible proportions but because we are astonished at its irreducible paradoxes and revel in playing with them. On the downside, though, some of us frequently assume that our reading of the ocean's face and fringes will make do for a plumbing of its depths. Naturally, we take a dim view of those who prefer the uplands and the mountaintops. We can hardly be faulted for that: all of us love our own neighborhood best and instinctively distrust those who breathe other airs. Still, provincialism has to be watched carefully when we speak of an ocean into which all rivers flow — and of a God who, when he is lifted up from the earth in Jesus, draws *all* to himself.

But enough of that for now. On the grounds that those of us in the middle, upland airs are inevitably in frequent, if not always friendly, contact with both our sea-level and mountain top neighbors — and because the strengths and weaknesses of both groups tend to rub off on us — let me try, before turning to this second group, to characterize the thin-air breathers who occupy the highest provinces of all.

Those of us who have lived on the mountaintops for most of the century now so nearly and unlamentedly past — who have tended to rate reason above revelation and to deem ourselves the intellectual masters of Christian discourse — have put a great gulf between ourselves and our predecessors in the dialogue. For one obvious thing, we have deliberately moved ourselves farther from the ocean of Scripture than those before us. This change of habitat was understandable, of course: on the one hand, the fundamentalism of our erstwhile neighbors at the seaside was alarming, even repellent; on the other, the slash-and-burn tactics of the biblical critics we increasingly clasped to our bosom (form criticism, higher criticism, literary criticism, historical criticism) left many of us (especially those still infected with the virus of eighteenth-century deism) precious little reason to see Scripture as any personal revelation of God at all. And so, in the thin air of these higher colonies, there rushed into the Scripture-starved void we thus created — as into the man out of whom a single demon was cast — an abundance of fabulous beasts that has made our last state worse than our first.

Just think of the bestiary of intellectual "-isms" which have long since replaced the old donkeys and workhorses that once labored at theological formulation and biblical interpretation. Liberalism, modernism, positivism, empiricism, logical positivism, postmodernism, and deconstructionism for seven others; and the death of God, feminist theology, womanist theology, the theology of liberation, and semeiotics for an extra handful. I'm far from saying that these are, one and all, nasty beasts — or even that any of them is an unqualified menace. But our preoccupation with such creatures of air and darkness — our allowing them to ramp and roar over the whole of the theological enterprise and distract us from any meaningful grappling with the scriptural deposit itself — has been, to put it as mildly as possible, a not unmixed blessing. Especially since the point of the free-for-all thus encouraged has more and more become not the search for truth but the extermination of whatever beast preceded our latest monster into the melee. To change the metaphor, what happened was that we allowed philosophical house-wrecking to replace theological home-building as the principal joy of academe.

On the bright side, there were some redeeming features in all this. There was certainly enthusiasm, and there was even a bit of astonishment in our intellectual beast-handling. But the enthusiasm was mostly destructive, the innocent bystanders frequently got bitten, and our astonishment seldom felt free enough to hunt for its true quarry in the bizarreness of the Gospel beast itself. On the gloomy side, therefore, what we have brought forth in the upper airs of Christian intellectualism is a preference for theological prolegomena over theological product, for debating not the issues but the shape of the negotiating table — for an interminable kaffeeklatsch on the porch of theology instead of an exploration of the house of faith.

But enough of that, too. Time now to turn to those of us in the middle airs — to those in the sprawling and varied terrain that lies between the two habitats I've characterized (or, if you like, stigmatized) so far. As with all who try to occupy a middle ground, our virtues here can all too easily be seen as vices — or, if we are lucky, vice versa. Consider the confusion of our condition. To take but one example: Some of us here live closer to fundamentalism than the rest, some closer to liberalism; but there is hardly a beast from either of the other two territories that you cannot find kept here as a house pet or allowed to run loose and leave unwanted deposits on other people's lawns. For all our confusion, however, we do have one grand distinction: *we do at least make an effort to live with each other* — an effort, incidentally, that our ragged but real presence as a buffer between our higher and lower neighbors graciously absolves them from making. They can simply despise each other; we are obsessed by a desire to get along.

They, of course, see us as hopeless compromisers attempting to negotiate a political truce between irreconcilable intellectual opposites. But we reject that caricature. We even have a few among us who can portray our bumpy *via media* — our grand amalgam of contradictions — as an almost holy hint of the synthesis of opposites that lies at the heart of all great truths. They will even make bold to point out that such a taste for paradox is not a bad attitude with which to start in on the Gospel. We see ourselves, therefore, as the "anglicans" (with a small "a") of Christian discourse. We are willing to waffle about what other people tell us are unqualified exigencies. We would rather see everyone have at least an Eggo to pop in the toaster than to starve the half or so of us who cannot and will not eat artichokes.

We legalize the ordination of women, for example, and then go blithely on allowing those who cannot stomach it to refuse to practice it. We tolerate both those who bless homosexual unions and those who curse them. We live with biblical literalists in the hope that they will see the error of their ways, and with "gender-neutral-language" enthusiasts in the hope, perhaps, that God will eventually "give them repentance and better minds." We are, in short, the politicians of Christian discourse. Even the caricature, you see, we turn into a virtue.

But we do have one utterly crippling debility that we have yet to recognize, one lack that even our ideological neighbors do not see because they suffer from it too: *we are as bereft of "Gospel-centered" astonishment as they are.* Worse yet, where they have at least passion, we are so busy balancing that we have next to none. Theology among us has been reduced to tasting everything on the menu and ending up with intellectual indigestion. We are so busy sampling the predictable little quiches and crudités on the academic buffet that we have ruined our appetite for the startling flavors and large portions of the Supper of the Lamb. And as for preaching? Well, preaching among us has far too often turned into the mere dispensing of advice. Even worse, the advice we hand out consists of little more than exhortations about a host of supposedly achievable life-enhancements, without even once getting our hearers within shouting distance of the astounding gift that's been handed us in Jesus at the price of no human accomplishment whatsoever. Our pulpits are fountains of irrelevancy when they are not puddles of dullness. They soak us with helpful hints about self-improvement in everything from morality, to spirituality, to health, to family life, to peace of mind — all the way down the ladder of the unaccomplishable to the ultimate banality: the advice that if we are loving, we will find the key to earthly happiness.

And all the while, every last item in that farrago of free advice is a hundred-eighty degrees off the Gospel mark. Jesus proclaims unlimited forgiveness, not the excoriation of sinners. He hands out the resurrection of the body, not spiritual perfection in some alien heaven. He comes to us in the brokenness of our health, in the shipwreck of our family lives, in the loss of all possible peace of mind, even in the very thick of our sins. He saves us *in* our disasters, not *from* them. He emphatically does not promise to meet only the odd winner of the self-improvement lottery; he meets us all in our endless and inescapable losing. And as for the Great White Queen of Advice — the suggestion that love will make life come up roses here and now — well, according to the Gospel, love is just a recipe for getting yourself crucified. But not only is all such advice demonstrable malarkey; it's mere pandering to a market that the Gospel has no interest in pleasing. It's what the world thinks it wants to hear, not what God in Christ has to tell it. But most of all, it is to yawn. It is to lull the world to sleep and invite it to dream of a world that advice can never in a million years create.

All is not lost, however. Even though the lines dividing conservatives, moderates, and liberals may once have been drawn between the churches, they now run inside everybody's church. Among us there are liberal Baptists, white-wine Methodists, fundamentalist Anglicans, High Church Lutherans, and Low Church Roman Catholics — and you can paste any of those ideological bus designations on any other churches you like and still find goodly companies of riders glad to get on. At the moment, to be sure, it seems that marking your bus conservative will get you the most (or at least the most vocal) passengers. But one of the rules of history is that another bus will always be along soon. Ideological fads come and go: in an age plagued by the unpredictabilities of church-shopping, it would be unwise to presume too much on the loyalty of any momentary ridership.

From what I've said so far, you can no doubt catch a hint of where I'm going. As I continue to characterize the current bankruptcy of the church, I shall portray the various episodes of it as subspecies of a single, overarching poverty. That poverty, to say it again, is our almost total loss of the astonishment which alone can be the taproot of Christian enthusiasm, not to mention of Christian intellectualism. We have forfeited that *fascination with strangeness* which alone can enable us to do justice to the strange God of the strange Scriptures whom we, as the strangest of all possible religious institutions, must represent to the world. And when I come finally to suggest how we can get out of the lamentable Chapter Eleven condition we're now in, everything I shall urge upon us will boil down to a recovery of the coin of that astonishment.

But since the heart of Christian astonishment is the mind-boggling goodness of the Good News — and since the sheer *fun* of the Gospel is the other side of the coin of our astonishment at it — let me make one last observation about all of us. Whether we are conservatives, moderates, or liberals, *we are no fun at all.* Watching us as conservatives is about as much fun as watching cement harden. Watching us as middle-grounders is less fun than waiting for a can of worms to make up its mind. And watching us as liberals? Well, watching a wrecker's ball at work is fun of sorts — until you realize that no landmark building has the smallest chance of surviving the enthusiasm of the demolition experts. (You will note, I hope, that I haven't taken sides in my analysis so far. I've studiously included Christians of all stripes in a single, comprehensive "us" — and I've tried to avoid turning anyone into a despised "them." I agree with Pogo: "We have met the enemy and they are us.")

What we most need, therefore, is not to decide which ideological bus is the vehicle of the future but to stop trying to decide anything of the sort, and then to look long enough and hard enough at our history to come to an understanding of the disastrous excursions on which all previous and present buses have taken us. But since I've insisted on that point several times already, let's get on with the job in earnest — beginning with a look, from Moses onward, at the three different models of the Israelite bus that the people of God tried out in the course of their journey. Even before the Christian enterprise got going, you will discover, the forms of ecclesiastical transportation developed a habit of breaking down.

3. The Church
before the Church

For most of the historical reflections and some of the other ideas in this chapter, I'm indebted to the Old Testament scholar Walter Brueggemann and his article entitled "Rethinking Church Models through Scripture." If I've bent any of his theses beyond recognition, I apologize to him; otherwise, I'm an unrepentant borrower.

▼   ▼   ▼

Even though Christians have commonly assumed that the principal, if not the divinely revealed, form of Israel's life before the Common Era was the state-church model that flourished from the time of David to the Babylonian Captivity (circa 1,000 to 587 B.C.E.), that's not the case historically. There are two other and very different forms — one before the Davidic Monarchy and one from the Captivity onward — which, now that the Christendom model of the church has broken down, have far more to teach us than the Monarchy-Temple form does. To be sure, all through the medieval period (and especially at the time of the established churches in the nation-states of Europe), the kingly-priestly model fitted like a glove. Even at the coronation of Queen Elizabeth II, the choir still sang the anthem "Zadok the priest and Nathan the prophet anointed Solomon King."

But those days are now well and truly gone, and it's time to take a much closer look at the models of Israel's life that preceded and followed the Monarchy. Not that the state-church form of Judaism will ever go completely into the historical discard. For one thing, it is the model that organizes and even dominates the text itself of the Hebrew Scriptures. For another, it provided the early church with the concept of the Davidic Messiah that lay at the heart of its proclamation about Jesus: "Therefore let the entire house of Israel know with certainty that God has made him both Lord and Messiah, this Jesus whom you crucified" (Acts 2:36). Still, so little else in our present context corresponds to that model that most of its baggage no longer has any relevance for us. Therefore, now that we're faced with the necessity of shopping for a new form of the church, it's high time to look at what the other versions of the community of faith in the Hebrew Scriptures may have to teach us.

My first job in this chapter will be to give you a sketch of each of the three models in the order in which they appeared. After that, I'll try to evaluate them briefly along the lines laid down in my first chapter — specifically, to say how and to what extent they qualified as *religion,* as *institutional structures,* and as vehicles for the proclamation of a *catholic* (universal) salvation. On with it, then.

The band of slaves who were liberated from Egypt by the Passover and at the Red Sea — and who, during the wilderness wanderings and in the meeting at Sinai first found their identity as the people of Yahweh (the LORD), the God of Abraham, Isaac, and Jacob — were not at all what they later became. To begin with, they were not a "religious group." Rather, they were a community knit together by the retelling of the *story of their deliverance* by God. One way of putting it would be to say that while they had a *liturgy* (meaning an identity-affirming proclamation of their communal history), they did not have a *religion* (meaning a developed set of creedal, cultic, and ethical requirements that created their identity). In short, they were indeed a community under God; but almost all the further details of their life as a community were still to be decided.

Soon enough, of course, the people of the Exodus (circa 1250 to 1000 B.C.E.) acquired the Torah, the covenanted Law of God, in which those details were spelled out and by which they became something of a religious community. But they had an odd religion

— what with their imageless, unnameable, ambulatory God and their lack of any real estate of their own on which to worship him. In this last respect, the religion they had was quite unlike the religions of the Canaanite peoples among whom they found themselves. The gods of the *goyim* were strictly local deities, more like mayors than celestial beings: if you moved to a new place, you gave your worship to a new god. The people of the God of Israel, on the other hand, took the view that their portable deity was the only rightful God of every place — despite the fact that, in defiance of the god-rules, he dwelt in an empty space, between two statues, on a shelf over a box, in a tent inside a tent, which was constantly being set up and taken down as they moved about. And while they did indeed worship that God with many of the trappings of religion (the book of Leviticus, if you like, being the part of the Torah that most spells out their religion's *cultic* requirements, and the book of Deuteronomy being the part that stresses its *ethical* and *creedal* aspects), it couldn't have looked like much of a religion to the folks who had the bad luck to run afoul of it. An excuse for poaching on other people's property, yes. A pretext for conquest, yes. An exercise in theological chutzpah, yes. But a respectable religion? Not a chance.

The same thing is true of the *institutional* status of the people of the Exodus: they had none. They were a profoundly marginal group, without any of the apparatus of an organized society — no stable social structures, no bureaucracy, no treasury, no intelligentsia, and no prophetic voices — just the Torah, a tent, and whatever happened next. They had about as much institutional structure as street theater: lots of improvisation, plenty of borrowing and stealing from whomever they bumped into, and free adaptation of other people's ideas and property for their own purposes; but precious little polity, and no property at all. True enough, the people of the Exodus eventually stumbled into the ad hoc administrative system depicted in the book of Judges; but that was less an institutional arrangement than it was, as Loren Mead observes, "a system of crisis-management that never worked satisfactorily." As I've said, it was a *liturgical* rather than an institutional community: its chief concern (and its greatest achievement) was to voice and revoice, to act and re-enact, the *story* of what it was all about.

But nothing stands still. Improvisational acting groups either pass away or become legitimate (or at least off-Broadway) theater. So too with Israel in the following period under the Monarchy. Since its liturgical show did not fold but actually managed to get theater space of its own with the conquest of Jerusalem, the temptations to institutional and religious respectability were impossible to resist. The people begged Samuel, for example, to appoint a king to govern them "like other nations." But Samuel, old-line liturgical community type that he was, thought that was a terrible idea. He even gave them a list of all the institutional horrors it would let them in for: taxation, conscription, a standing army spoiling for war, and expropriation of personal property by the rule of eminent domain. "You will cry out because of your king," Samuel told them, "but the LORD will not answer you in that day" — because, he insisted, they were rejecting not just him but the God who brought them up out of Egypt and whom they had worshiped in the liturgical recitation of that deliverance. God, apparently, agreed. Eventually, though, both the LORD and Samuel caved in and gave them Saul for their first king.

From there on it was straight down the institutional hill and right into the state-church model. It ceased to seem odd to the formerly landless and polity-lacking people of the Exodus that they should have priests who could meddle in the palace and kings who could go hog-wild over matters of religion. And so it became increasingly difficult for either the state or the church to conceive of itself as separable from the other. A kind of symbiosis developed between them — a mutual dependence so profound that the "established religion" model it generated could be broken only by a catastrophe from the outside. But that gets us ahead of the story. For now, we need to look a bit more closely at the monarchical institution's itch to become a *religion* in earnest.

The LORD may have objected to the idea of religion strenuously enough to keep David from converting the tent of witness into a "house made with hands"; but with Solomon, the project was accomplished. He built the Temple. Out of stone. In Jerusalem. And pretty much with all the fixings of the stock religions of the time. True enough, the liturgy of the Exodus community still played a considerable part in Israel's life; but if you read the books of Samuel, Kings, and Chronicles, you will see that it was the business of religion — and of a state religion, no less — that was the primary focus of attention. The Temple and its priesthood became an agency of civic leadership, just as the Monarchy increasingly involved itself in the affairs of religion. That in doing so the kings of Israel and Judah frequently bought into the idolatrous religions of the *goyim* was, historically speaking, a minor glitch. The major disaster was that it was a case of the fisherman's joke on the fish all over again: *religion as such* had become the hook buried in the bait of the religious practices the kings adopted — the religious practices of the Temple not excepted. You don't buy competing brands of a product unless you've already assumed they're essentially the same thing as the product you've been using. You can't change your religion unless you're convinced you had one to begin with.

Two more institutional features of the monarchical model of Judaism, and we're ready to move on. The first was the rise of an *intelligentsia* — of the *sages* represented by the book of Proverbs and similar writings. A stable social order gives savvy people the leisure to spread their mental wings. And so while the sages went along with the Temple religion, they felt increasingly free to let their intellectual interests flow in the direction of moral and political philosophy — into the totally new realm of worldly wisdom. Hence the sometimes extensive passages of secular free advice in the Hebrew Scriptures that may have had their origin in this period — and the superior, even elitist tone that the giving of such advice often lends to its dispensers' utterances.

Far more important, though, was the appearance at this time of the *prophets*. When the people of the Exodus were rattling around in the desert, they found a lot of problems to complain about — the hardships of the journey, the loss of Egyptian home-cooking, and their disenchantment with the high-handedness of Moses, to mention only a few. But in all their long list of wilderness gripes, it never occurred to them to include the peccadilloes and shortcomings of an institutional structure. Prophecy against a system, you see, cannot arise until there is a system to prophesy against — and not until both the prophets and the targets of their criticism have agreed that the system is worth a damn. It was this commitment to *the same conversation,* to a dialogue that both sides thought mattered, that led the prophets to find their witness necessary and the kings to find their irritation with it justified. Fascinatingly, the period of the great prophets (Isaiah, Amos, Hosea, Jeremiah) does not begin until the monarchical establishment is in place — and it ends abruptly when that establishment collapses. Which brings us, nicely, to the third and final model of the community of faith in the Hebrew Scriptures.

As I've already noted, only a deathblow from the outside could put an end to the monarchical period's conversation between kings, priests, intelligentsia, and prophets. That blow, historically speaking, was not long in coming. After a mere four hundred years (in 597 B.C.E.), King Nebuchadnezzar of Babylon captured Jerusalem, sacked the Temple, and deported King Jehoiachin of Judah, along with the cream of the establishment, to Babylon. Not long after that (in 589, with the rebellion of Zedekiah, the next and last king of Judah before the Exile), the Babylonians devastated Jerusalem; and in 587, they finally sacked the city itself and deported the significant remainder of the population. The period of the Exile had begun in earnest. The establishment model, cut off from its roots, was forced (as the Psalmist says) to "sing the LORD's song in a strange land" — a necessity which, by the exigencies of history and the resourcefulness of the Jewish people, led them not only to a new song but to the creation of yet another model of their common life.

Hence the third development: the emergence (in the exilic and postexilic periods and on into the periods of Persian dominance, Greek hegemony, and eventually Roman rule) of the model of Judaism that in many respects continues to this day. The people of God who in the wilderness had ordered their life around the Exodus liturgy — and who in the monarchical period had become an establishment complete with temple, kings, priests, sages, and prophets — now became a *people of the book.* It was in this era that the Hebrew Scriptures finally took on the shape they now have. And thus it was in this era that the *text,* and not the Temple, became the cornerstone of Jewish identity.

Consider the forces that were at work. To begin with, take prophecy. The Jews of the Exile no longer had any significant influence over public policy. They were sometimes tolerated by the Babylonians, sometimes despised; but they remained, through the whole period, politically irrelevant. There were no budding Amoses to inveigh against the state establishment, for the simple reason that the state hadn't the least interest in conversing with them. Even Jeremiah, who began his career before the Exile with old-style diatribes against the kings, officials, priests, and prophets of the house of Israel, changed his tune during the Exile. In place of his legendary jeremiads, he settled at first for words of comfort to his people in their tribulations, and then he went on to invent an entirely new message: one of *hope.* And it was that note of hope — that insistence on a mysterious, hidden future about to be revealed — that was the bedrock of the apocalyptic style of prophecy that now was about to replace the old establishment-oriented one. To someone like the writer of the book of Daniel, the status quo ante of the monarchical institution hardly mattered because the status quo post had become all that counted. Apocalyptic is a prophetic voice for the marginalized, not for those who think they are in a position to do something effective about the culture. Like the phoenix, it arises only among those who sit in the ashes of collapse.

On the other hand, take the matter of the *preservation of Jewish identity* during and after the Exile. Under the Monarchy it had not been a problem. There may have been temptations, as always, to wander off in the direction of other religions; but the institutional structures of the Temple-palace establishment — and the payoffs for going along with them — were quite sufficient to keep the self-awareness of the people of Israel intact. The period of the third model of Judaism, however, provided no such buttresses. The social pressure on the Jews was always, subtly or not so subtly, not to be Jews. It was to conform to a powerful, often attractive, and above all rewarding or punishing Gentile environment. In that world, if a Jew went to a Greek health club, he would be so embarrassed by his circumcision that he would do all he could to conceal it.

So how *did* the Jews of the Exile preserve their identity? As I've already said, they did it first by embracing the *hope for the future* that was the stock-in-trade of their apocalyptic literature: *God* was in charge of their identity, and his plans for it were already hidden in the works, waiting to be revealed in the last days. But that was not all. At the same time, they went to work on the text of Scripture itself and included in it the identity-confirming stories of their roots that can most easily be seen in the first and perhaps the best known of the books of the Bible. The Jews of the Exodus may have been aware of Abraham, for example, but they didn't have the book of Genesis as the Jews of the postexilic period now produced it. That book is an exilic/postexilic creation. It's a leap backward into "prehistory" designed to provide what was by now becoming a *community of the text* (not just a people reciting a liturgy) with the paradigmatic origins of their true identity.

But, for a final point, they hung the whole weight of their identity on the *text itself.* Not only did they formulate that text as we now have it (the time of the Exile and afterward is most likely the period of the final editing of the Hebrew Scriptures); they took up the *interpretation* of the text as the task that lay closest to the bone of their identity. Most notably of all, it was during this period that the *Synagogue* was first invented — and it was now that the Synagogue replaced the Temple as the center, for all practical purposes, of Jewish life. *Tradition* replaced institution as the binding force; and the rabbis, who became the expounders of that tradition, replaced the priests and prophets as the authenticating voices of Judaism. As a matter of fact, it was during the Exile that the people of Israel began to develop the *family* rituals (the Seder, for example) which they would carry into the Diaspora. True enough, the Temple was rebuilt in 520 B.C.E. and lasted as an institution for the next half-millennium. But it was never again the chief root of the people's connectedness. It might even be said that the Jews didn't really *need* to go back to Jerusalem to make their way into the future; in Babylon, they had already invented all the tools they needed for the trip. Their return to Jerusalem to rebuild the Wall and the Temple was not so much a necessity as it was a *metaphor:* it was less a return to the womb of their past than it was a road map leading them into a future that would eventually manifest itself in Zionism. Indeed, when the Temple was finally destroyed by the Romans in 70 C.E., the Synagogue and the household rituals had so thoroughly over-shadowed it in the popular imagination that it was never built again. It simply wasn't missed enough. Judaism went right on being Judaism without so much as a hiccup. The *story* had once again become everything, the institution next to nothing.

Obviously, the history of Israel as I've sketched it so far has a good deal of relevance to the history of the Christian enterprise. The church of the New Testament began as the same kind of liturgical community as the one that lived by the Exodus narrative; and over the years it developed into something that was almost a dead ringer for the monarchical state church. But in our time, all the institutional structures by which we've identified ourselves have either come down around our ears or are threatening to do so shortly. It may well turn out, therefore, that in our present condition we might profitably take several pages from the model of community that arose in postexilic Judaism.

As I proceed through the argument of this book, I shall take whatever opportunities present themselves to apply the lessons of Israel's experience to that of the church. At this point, however, I want to make a brief checklist — a kind of ecclesiastical report card, if you will — of the scores achieved by the people of the Old Covenant on the tests that I shall be using when I come to grade the church of the New Testament. I've already said that our problems as Christians stem from the fact that we too are a community that was neither a religion, nor an institution, nor a state church, nor a corporation, but that we too have turned ourselves, at one time or another, into all of the above. I've also said that the *catholicity* of the community of the Gospel is, in all times and places, its most endangered species. How did the people of Israel do on those tests?

Take the category of *religion* first. For the period of the *Exodus,* I give them a (generous) B+. To begin with, they hardly conceived of themselves as having a religion at all. And even though they eventually acquired religious practices of sorts, it was the story of their deliverance from Egypt, not the ceremonials of their religion, that remained the center of their identity. It was what God had done for them, not what they could con God into doing by their sacrifices and offerings, that was uppermost in their minds. For the period of the *Monarchy,* though, I give them an F. They turned themselves into a religion in spades. Getting their religion right — and, above all, achieving the satisfaction of having gotten it right — became their defining activity. The story of their history was pretty much elbowed into the background by the history of their religious preoccupations. But for the time of the *Exile* and afterwards, I give them an A-. They downplayed the religiosity of the Temple model and reinvented their story as not only a liturgical activity but also a textual treasure — and it is that story, I think, along with the assorted commentaries on it, that remains the definition of their identity right up to the present. The common life of a people is defined not so much by their doing the same thing at the same time (twenty million Americans watching a rerun of *NYPD Blue* are not a community) as it is by bearing in their bones the astonishing story of who they were and what they are. Judaism since the Exile has hardly been a religion at all; it has been a *people.* And even if some of its people have "lost their religion" entirely, they are still *the people of God.*

Institutional status next. *Exodus model:* an A. Cursed (or blessed) with no status whatsoever, they never got around to being any kind of institution at all — and therefore never contracted any of the institutional diseases that later plagued them. *Monarchy-Temple model:* D-. They became as institutional as any group that ever came down the pike; I spare them the indignity of an F only because they never quite forgot the story of who they were. *Postexilic model:* an A here too. Once again, their marginality precluded their using institutional status as the basis for defining their identity; even the institutions that they did allow to drag on faded in importance as the power of the text grew and flourished in their lives.

Finally, *catholicity.* Since this is definitely a Christian concept, it may be a bit of a jolt for you to hear it applied to the people of Israel. But I think it can be justified, so watch.

The *Exodus model* gets a C+. The odd identity of the Jews as people of a story was fragile enough to require rather a lot of exclusivity and a great deal of mayhem against their enemies. Nevertheless, their equally odd identity as the people of a God who laid claim to literally the whole earth gave them at least a leg up on universality. And then there's Exodus 12:38: "A *mixed multitude* also went up with them, and very many cattle, both flocks and herds." Not only does that ring the bell of diversity rejoiced in; its reference to cattle, flocks, and herds anticipates the astonishing catholicity of God's parting shot in the last verse of the book of Jonah: "And should I not be concerned about Nineveh, that great city, in which there are more than a hundred and twenty thousand persons who do not know their right hand from their left, and also many animals?" Come to think of it, I'll raise that grade for catholicity from a C+ to a B-: they didn't do all that badly.

The *Monarchy-Temple model,* though, gets yet another F. Defending the boundaries of a religious institution is the world's fastest way to forget that the God it represents is genuinely concerned with the world beyond the institution.

The *postexilic model,* however, has to settle for a mere B+ here. The people of Israel in this period did indeed glimpse for themselves a catholic mission (Israel was to be "a light to the *nations*"). They were even able to see the hand of God actively at work in people who weren't Jews. In Second Isaiah they came up with the astonishing notion that Cyrus the Persian was the chosen agent of God for their deliverance from Babylon — that he was in fact "Yahweh's Anointed": his *Messiah,* no less. And in Zechariah they even caught a hint of the remarkable idea that the ultimate fulfillment of Israel's purpose will be that "many nations shall join themselves to the LORD on that day, and shall be my people." Still, the same struggle to survive that led the Exodus community to think in terms of "us against them" made it hard for postexilic Judaism to go all the way to the implicit and uncompromising catholicity of God's covenant with Abraham: ". . . in you, *all the families of the earth* shall be blessed."

That job was to be the work of yet a fourth model of Judaism — which, I shall make bold to insist, is *the church of the early New Testament period.* If you will now bear with me into the next chapter, I even think I can prove it to you.

4. The Church from Peter through Paul

Before we take up the early Jerusalem model of the church, I want to underscore something I said at the beginning of this book. The models that the church uses to give form to its life and understand its identity always come from *the social and cultural context* in which the church finds itself at any given time and place. They are not handed to it directly by God (though his people have frequently explained or justified them that way), nor are they to be found in any prescriptive sense in Scripture (though that too has often been put forth as their source). This last point can easily be proved. Of the three models of the "church" in the Hebrew Scriptures, the first two (the *Exodus-liturgy model* and the *Monarchy-Temple model*) came out of contexts in which the people of Israel had none, or only some, of those Scriptures as we now have them — and the third (the *exilic/postexilic model*) arose while the present shape of the Hebrew Scriptures was in the process of formation.

Much the same thing is true of the first model of the church in the New Testament. While "the believers" who made up the Jerusalem church did indeed by then have the full text of the Hebrew Scriptures, they had (in 35 C.E., say) not a scrap of the New Testament as it now exists. Accordingly, I'm going to hold that the forms they chose as a model for their life came quite naturally out of the whole corpus of the Jewish Scriptures — and even more naturally out of the postexilic model of Judaism in the midst of which it found itself living. Once again, the simplest way to put it is this: if, ten days after Pentecost, you had asked Peter, James, and John what their religion was, they would have informed you, quite plainly, that they were Jews. The book of Acts (2:46-47) states that "they spent much time together in the Temple . . . praising God and having the goodwill of all the people." At the very same time, you see, they were both accepted adherents of Judaism and faithful proclaimers of Jesus their Lord and Messiah as the fulfillment of Judaism. They did not, at that point, think of themselves as Christians.

While you may find that odd, it's not unusual. If you study history, the tendency of movements within institutions to remain within the institutions that were their first home fairly leaps out at you. Luther began his reform movement inside the Western, Latin church and only later felt it necessary to separate from it. Likewise, Methodism arose as a movement to wake up the eighteenth-century Church of England; it was a while before the "chapel meeting" system of the early Methodists finally became a separate church. And, for perhaps the closest parallel of all, I have it on good authority that in present-day Islam, there are believers in Christ who continue to be practicing Muslims.

One note. Nothing I've said about the primacy of context as the source of models for the church's life in any way prevents us from seeing the hand of God in the context or from holding that the Scriptures are the Word of God. If God is genuinely the Lord of history, then *context* can just as appropriately be ascribed to divine providence as it can be to the interplay of social, cultural, and economic forces. Indeed, if it's truly *history* that he's Lord of, those "secular" forces will be the very things he'll use, in all their developments and collisions, to tip his hand and express his Word. It's important to add, however, that in both Scripture and the church's life, God the Holy Spirit presides over the historical process *mysteriously,* not ham-fistedly: he lets events take their natural course and still gets the results he wants. In short, *he rides the bicycle of history home no-hands.* Think about that. God uses Cyrus the Persian to liberate the people of Israel from Babylon, even though Cyrus himself does nothing but his own thing for his own reasons. God saves the world through his Incarnate Word in Jesus by the historical accident of a judicial murder. And even though the Holy Spirit leaves the writers of the Bible free to say whatever comes into their unique and independent heads, he still manages to get from them the historical Scriptures he wants us to have as his Word written. Freedom in no way precludes providence, and providence has no need to interfere with freedom. (By the way: as for me — and for the record — I firmly believe that the Holy Scriptures of the Old and New Testaments are indeed the Word of God and that they contain all things necessary to salvation. But for all that, I also think we have them in all their saving grandeur as the result of quite unvarnished historical processes.)

But back to the Jerusalem church. As I said, it had the entire history of Israel (and thus all three forms of Judaism in the Hebrew Scriptures) to draw on when it came to model its self-identity. Consider the *Exodus-liturgy model.* The people of Israel never lost sight of it, even in the midst of their succeeding forms. The annual celebration of the Passover was precisely an ongoing sacrament of liberating power — a *re-presentation,* a real *making present again* — of the historical mystery of deliverance by which God had first made some refugees from Egypt his chosen people. God's action in the Passover, you see, was never simply one that began and ended; it's an action that *continues.* It has never forsaken its historical roots; but it has never gone even halfway into the shade of the past — not during the Monarchy, and not in all the time since. And the same is true of the *marginality* of the Exodus model. While it was indeed overshadowed for a while by the institutional successes of the monarchical model, it continued to be operative, full force, throughout both the Monarchy and the postexilic period that followed it.

So too with the early church model. The core members of the Jerusalem church, who had kept the Passover with Jesus on the night before he died, were themselves speedily marginalized by the Jewish establishment. Two of the scriptural models of Jewish self-identity, therefore, fell nicely into their lap. From the *Exodus model,* they learned to see themselves as the proclaimers of liberation — to see Jesus, that is, as the *Paschal Lamb,* and to see in him *the very same deliverance,* this time from the bondage of sin and death, that their ancestors had experienced in their release from the bondage of Egypt. And from the *monarchical model,* they laid hold of the concept of the *Messiah,* the *Davidic King* who would be the fulfillment of Israel's destiny, and promptly fastened it on Jesus. If I've spoken in mostly disapproving terms of the period of the Monarchy, I have to take back at least something of that here. Even after the actual Davidic institution had gone pretty much into the discard historically, it still continued to have a hold on the Jewish imagination — and, more importantly, to be in many ways the integrating theme of the completed text of Scripture. So it was as natural as breathing for the early church to see Jesus as the fulfillment of the messianic hope of Israel and to proclaim him as "both Lord and *Christ.*" But what was truly inspired (and controversial) about their proclamation was that they made it in the face of the fact that, judged on the basis of previous messianic expectations, *Jesus was a failed Messiah.* He *died* (which was something the Messiah wasn't supposed to do); and he *changed nothing historically* (unless you could believe the bizarre claim that he had repaired all of history mysteriously). In a word, from the quite unparadoxical model of Monarchy and Temple, the early church plucked the unlikely rose of paradox and made it the centerpiece of the church's identity.

By historical necessity, however, the early church's only living, available source for all its models of identity and structure was the form of Judaism in which it lived: the postexilic, *community-of-the-text model.* That, if you will, was the *governing* context for the earliest believers. The text of the Hebrew Scriptures now stood before them in its fullness. And it was from that lived-in and commented-upon text that they shaped their life as a community. It was from that text, not from any actual experience of the Monarchy, that they took the expectation of a messianic man on horseback and converted it into their paradoxical proclamation of Jesus as the Christ. And it was from that text, not from having lived through the Exodus themselves, that they received the *story* of their liberation and the liturgical style in which they celebrated and proclaimed their version of that story. They became a people of a new story and a new liturgy — which they took as nothing less than the fulfillment of the old story and the old liturgy: "They devoted themselves to the apostles' teaching and fellowship [that is, to the proclamation of the *Gospel*], to the breaking of bread [that is, to the *eucharistic* liturgy of their liberation], and to the prayers" (Acts 2:42). They saw themselves, in a word, as Israel all over again — as, at the most, the next model of Judaism.

Once again, they did not see themselves as Christians. The word "Christian" does not appear until the eleventh chapter of the book of Acts — and then only as a tag attached to them by outsiders. Nor does the notion that they were a new religion (or even a religion at all) seem to have occurred to them. The word "religion," in the sense of *sect,* is something they refused to apply to themselves. In the book of Acts, Paul denies that the church is a *haéresis,* a *secta,* a religious phenomenon in its own right. The Sadducees and the Pharisees were indeed sects, *haéreses* (see Acts 5:17 and 15:5) — that is, groups which espoused differing opinions on certain religious questions; but in Acts 24:14 Paul refuses to sit still for having "the Way" (namely, the church, the fellowship of the resurrection) seen as a particular *haéresis,* because for him the church is simply the fulfillment of Judaism. As a matter of fact, on the basis of Paul's "Law-grace" argument in Romans and Galatians (Abraham becomes a Jew not by the religion of the Law but by grace through faith), it even seems to me that it's the fundamentally *non-religious* character of Judaism itself that he has uppermost in mind when he denies the applicability of the word *haéresis* to the church.

In addition, besides not being a new religion, the early church was not an *institution:* what institutional form it did have was supplied by the Temple and the Synagogue. At the most, therefore, it was a typical movement within an already existing religion, not a new franchise setting up to market a religion of its own. That its members were quickly marginalized and persecuted by the Jewish establishment they felt themselves part of is one of the sadder facts of history. They did indeed develop an underdog mind-set and a vocabulary in which they became a believing "us" and the Jewish authorities became a feared "them." And that mind-set admittedly laid the groundwork for one of the saddest facts of Christian history:

the inveterate anti-Semitism that to this day has plagued the church and scourged the Jewish people. But for all that, the church did not, at that time, think of itself as a different religious shop entirely.

To see this more clearly, you have to look at the names the church gave itself in the book of Acts. Here they are, in the order of the declining frequency with which they appear:

"the brethren"	(*hoi adelphoí:* the brothers — now often translated "brothers and sisters" — 28 times)
"the disciples"	(*hoi mathētaí:* the disciples, the followers, the pupils, the learners — 22 times)
"the church"	(*hē ekklēsía:* the church, the assembly — 18 times)
"those of *the way*"	(*hē hodós:* the way, the path — 9 times)
"the believers"	(*hoi pisteúontes:* the believers, the faithful — 7 times)
"the fellowship"	(*hē koinonía:* the fellowship, the community — 1 time)

Because the title "the church" rapidly became the dominant name for the group that proclaimed the dead and risen Jesus as Lord and Christ — and because it has remained the commonest name for two thousand years — I want to give it most of my attention. But before I do that, here are a few comments on the rest of the list.

First, *the brethren.* Jesus used the word *adelphós* often enough during his ministry to give his disciples good reason to get in the habit of thinking of their relationship to one another as that of brothers and sisters (though the feminine form *adelphḗ* occurs less frequently in the New Testament because in Greek the masculine was commonly used for generic references and the feminine only for specifically female ones). In any case, the closeness of the relationship they shared in the early church, coupled with their sense that their closeness was a gift from God rather than their own doing, plus their very marginality within the Jewish establishment — all this easily led the early church to use a *familial* term when they spoke of who they were.

On the other hand, the word *adelphoi,* as it appears in the book of Acts, actually bears witness to the *unity* that the earliest believers felt they had with Judaism — a unity that a fair number of the Jews of the time, at least in the Diaspora, were in fact willing to concede. In the Synagogue on the Sabbath day in Pisidian Antioch (Acts 13), for example, the Synagogue leaders greet Paul and his entourage as *ándres adelphoi,* "men and brethren"; and Paul returns the compliment by using the identical form of address to them. He even continues in the same vein: he speaks to them of "our" fathers, and he puts the blame for the rejection of the "word of salvation" in Jesus as the Messiah not on Judaism as such but only on "those in Jerusalem and their rulers."

The disciples. Even more often, Jesus (and later, the Gospel writers) referred to his followers as *mathētai.* If there is any direct linkage between Jesus and early church nomenclature, this is probably it.

Those of *the way.* This seems to be a name the church did think up pretty much on its own. What it bears witness to, I think, is the already mentioned fact that the disciples conceived of themselves as a movement within a religion rather than as a religion or an institution in their own right. They didn't think of themselves as a "church" in the sense that the word later acquired. They were a community of proclamation, not an organizational entity. True enough, they soon (Acts 15) found reason to hold an institutional brainstorming session of sorts; but it remained for the rest of us to get from that humble beginning to the Inquisition, the Presbyterian General Assembly, and the Clergy Deployment Process.

The believers. Once again, this is a name that demonstrates the early church's grip on something essential. "The *believers*" were not a group advocating a clutch of plausible practices that would, if performed, turn them into an agency for straightening up the world. Rather, they were simply a community which *trusted* that all the agenting called for had already been done by God in Christ — and which lived only and entirely by that trust. It was Paul, of course, who kicked the football of faith between the theological uprights; but it was the earliest church that had run the ball on the ground to the point from which he scored.

The fellowship. Koinonía may show up only once in Acts, but in the epistles of Paul and John it occurs a dozen or more times, referring either to the church's fellowship with the risen Jesus or to the fellowship that the members of the church have with each other. It therefore complements the familial emphasis of "the brethren" with the notes of *voluntary association* and of *common life.* (Incidentally, that leads me to mention one other name for the church which, while it does not appear as such in Acts, fills up a good two columns in my Greek concordance: *the body of Christ* [*to sṓma tou Christoû*]. It is this title that moves both the *familial* and the *associational* notes of the church all the way upstairs. There are no bits and pieces of anything on earth, and certainly no people, more closely related to each other than are the members of a living body. You can lose a family member or a club member and still have the same institutional entity you had before. But if you lose your lungs, your liver, or your heart, you have nothing. For solid 24-karat *unity,* nothing beats the body as an illustration.)

But now, finally, *the church, hē ekklēsía.* Forget the usual, etymological explanation for the adoption of the word (from *ek,* out, and *kaleín,* to call — thus making the church a *called-out* group). There's a much more germane one, and I'll spell it out for you in steps.

Step one. In the Hebrew Scriptures, two major words are used to refer to the *congregation* of Israel, or the *assembly* of Israel — that is, to Israel itself as a *community.* They are *qahál* and *ēdah,* and they are used more or less interchangeably; but one or the other of them appears as the word of choice in certain books. In Exodus, for example, *ēdah* is preferred by a wide margin; in Chronicles, *qahál* gets the nod.

Step two. After 288-247 B.C.E., which is the time during the postexilic period when the Hebrew Scriptures were translated into Greek, that version came to be known as the Septuagint, abbreviated as the Roman number LXX. The "seventy" in those appellations derives from the fact that this version was the work of seventy (actually seventy-two) scholars who, according to legend, labored separately yet miraculously produced seventy identical versions. (At that point, Hebrew had still not ceased, as it had by the time of Jesus, to be a spoken language. But as it faded from use, the Greek of the LXX became more and more widely used. By the time you get to Paul, for example, you find him quoting Scripture from the LXX in full confidence that not only Gentiles but Jews as well will be able to understand his arguments.) In any case, that leads us to

Step three. In the LXX, two Greek words are used to translate *édah*, and *qahál: édah*, generally, is rendered *synagōgé*, and *qahál*, *ekklēsía*.

Step four. And therefore, when the early New Testament church cast about for a word with which to denominate itself as the fulfillment of the *community*, the *congregation*, the *assembly* of Israel as the people of God (indeed, as that same community), it had to make a choice: since it was by then beginning to think in Greek, it had to decide between *synagōgé* and *ekklēsía*. But since the word *synagōge* had been preempted by becoming the name of a specific institution within Judaism, that left them only *ekklēsía* with which to designate themselves as the community that fulfilled the destiny of Israel as a whole. Q.E.D.

Fascinatingly, of the eighteen occurrences of *ekklēsía* in Acts, three of them still bear witness to assemblies other than the New Testament church. In Acts 7:38, Stephen, the about-to-be martyr, speaks of the "*ekklēsía* in the desert" of Sinai (a phrase which the King James Version blithely translates as "the *church* in the wilderness"). And in 19:32 and 19:39, *ekklēsía* is used in two of the ordinary, secular senses it had in the Greek language of the time: in 19:32, it occurs in a reference to the riot caused by an Ephesian *ekklesía* (meaning an assembly of people in a certain trade); and in 19:39, in the phrase "lawful assembly," it refers to an *ennómō ekklēsía*, meaning a *court of law* in which the matter of the riot should properly be heard. More on this later, when we get to the church in the Greco-Roman world. Suffice it to say here that in the other fifteen occurrences of *ekklēsía* in Acts, the word is simply used in the same sense that it had in the LXX: that is, as the name for the *congregation* of Israel, of which the *ekklēsía* of the New Testament was the fulfillment. (That the English word "church" was used as the translation of *ecclesia* from the later Latin is another story. "Church" came to us from Old High German, which, by a long detour, got it from Late Greek, where it was a reference to "the *Lord's* house." In any case, it comes long after the early church — from a time, as you can well imagine, when the church was up to its eyebrows in real estate and all the other trappings of the institutional model.)

How then do I write the report card on the early Jerusalem church? On *religion,* I give them a B+. Mostly, they managed to avoid thinking of themselves as a religion; but they were kept from an A by certain religious thought-patterns they inherited from the ancient people of God they still took as their model. Even in the early chapters of Acts, there is rather a lot of talk about what people need to do to get themselves right — religious talk, that is — talk which, because it rather quickly got around to suggesting that the Gentiles couldn't be members of the church unless they first became practicing Jews, threatened (until Paul) to turn the church into just another religion.

On *institutional status,* I give them an A-. The minus is because they inevitably began to develop institutional structures of their own. They had officers (Apostles, Deacons); they had a chain of command that installed the Jerusalem church at the top and that led to Paul's being called on the carpet for not paying sufficient attention to it. And, as already mentioned, they even held a council that, true to the pattern of all such institutional conclaves, hemmed and hawed its way through the questions at issue not by solving them creatively but by fashioning a compromise that left everyone with rather less than his heart desired.

On *catholicity,* however, I give them a B-. That's not meant as a bad grade: they did manage to get the point that the Gentiles had somehow to be included in the church, and they did produce an essentially catholic if half-baked waffle for everyone to eat. But because they couldn't quite break out of the pattern of religious requirements (dietary ones, ethical ones), they insured that the seeds of religion would be wafted into the future of the church. Still, thanks to the appearance of an extremely diligent yardman in the Apostle Paul, the church would always have a lifetime supply of the weed-killing doctrine of universal grace, which, even if it was rarely used as energetically as it should have been, would always be on hand to restore the catholicity of the church's garden.

And so, at last, Paul himself. Of all the contextual forces that impinged on the early church, he is practically Mr. Context. The Jerusalem "believers" may have been Jewish to the core, but it remained for Paul to unveil to them (or invent for them, whichever you like) the notion of the catholicity of *Judaism itself.* But first we need to be clear about what he actually said on the subject. The matter over which the question of catholicity arose was specifically whether Gentiles who wished to join the church and accept Jesus as Lord and Christ had to be circumcised and to keep the whole Jewish law on top of that. The Jerusalem church crowd probably figured that if that's the way they did it, why shouldn't everybody else? Admittedly, by the time of the Council in Acts 15, they had come down from that high horse a bit, but they were still religiously walking it in the yard. It was left to Paul, therefore, to say uncompromisingly, "God forbid!"

We usually think that what he said was something like this: "The Jews may have become Jews by circumcision and the law; but the Gentiles become Christians by grace through faith." But that's not what he said. His actual argument was that the Gentiles became *Jews* by grace through faith — that they became, as he said, *"children of Abraham"* and *"the Israel of God."* But then, in one of the great theological end-runs of all time, he went on to prove that even the Jews themselves became Jews *by faith alone* — without either circumcision or the law. Going all the way back to Abraham, the father of the people of God, Paul pointed out in classic rabbinical style that Abraham, in whom *all the families of the earth* would be blessed, was accepted by God (see Romans 4, Galatians 3, and Genesis 12-15) *four hundred and thirty years before there was any law at all*

— on the basis of his simply *believing* in God's promise to him. Judaism itself, therefore, was a faith community before it became a religious one.

This was the root of the uncompromising catholicity proclaimed by Paul in Galatians and Romans. At the risk of repeating myself, no single religion — not even the religion ordained in the law for the chosen people — can ever be catholic. And it can't be because it creates a community restricted to some instead of a fellowship to be extended to all: only such-and-such people, doing such-and-such works, can belong. But the community of faith in the promise of God is meant precisely to include all because the promise is made to all nations. And faith is the only requirement that can be imposed without destroying catholicity because no community that requires specific human achievements for admission will ever be able to stomach the vast army of underachievers that faith lets in free. The church, therefore, must have no such work-oriented requirements. It is not a *transactional agency* through which God deigns to reward the cooperative with his cooperation; rather, it's a *simple fellowship of trust* in the universal work of the God who has promised to include everybody. For Paul, the church was to be the "sacrament" of the fulfillment of that promise in Jesus — and it was to be just as catholic as Israel was meant to be from the start. It was to see itself as the ongoing sign of a salvation so all-encompassing that it would apply to anyone and everyone the church might ever run into. As a matter of fact, in the epistles to the Ephesians and the Colossians, Paul himself (or some successor, if you prefer that view of their authorship) made an astonishing leap backward in time and maintained that this salvation — this abrahamic choosing of people beyond the pale of Judaism — was not a transaction at all but a mystery that had been at work *before the foundation of the world.* It was not an insertion of something into history but part of the very constitution of history itself.

A short detour here for two notes — one on faith and the other on my use of the word "sacrament" in describing the church.

Faith first. Faith doesn't do anything; it simply enables us to relate ourselves to someone else who has already done whatever needs doing. Illustration: Imagine that I am in the hospital, in traction, with casts on both arms and both legs. And imagine further that every time you visit me, I carry on despairingly about the fact that my house, in my absence, is falling apart: the paint is peeling, the sills are rotting, the roof is blowing away in the wind.

But then imagine that one day, after a considerable interval, you come to me and say, "Robert, I have just paid off the contractor I engaged to repair your house. It's all fixed — a gift from me to you." What are my choices in the face of such good news? I cannot go out of the hospital to check for myself — I cannot *know* that you have fixed my house for me. I can only disbelieve you or believe you. If I disbelieve you, I go on being a miserable bore. But if I believe you — if I *trust* your word that you have done the job for me — I have my first good day in a long while. My faith, you see, accomplishes nothing but my own enjoyment.

Look at it another way. Suppose I had decided, while staring at the hospital ceiling, that if only I could work up enough faith, you would undertake to repair my house. And suppose further that I had grunted and groaned through every waking hour trying to get my faith meter up to red hot. What good would that have done unless *you* had decided, as a gift to me in response to no activity on my part whatsoever, to do the job for me? No good, that's what. Faith doesn't fix houses — carpenters and painters do. And faith doesn't pay bills, either. Faith, therefore, is not a gadget by which I can work wonders. It is just *trust in a person* who actually can work them — and who has promised me he already has.

Sacrament next. By sacrament, I mean a real presence, under a particular sign in a particular time and place, of something that's already present everywhere. It's not just a de novo production of that something or a mental reminder of that something, but the same old something itself present under a renewable sign. Take a kiss between two lovers: it's not some third thing that merely represents their love; it's their whole, already present love, re-presented — made really present again — at a specific point under a specific sign.

The Eucharist, for example (to take the highest view of it), is precisely a sacrament. It's not a transaction — not the mixing up of a fresh batch of the body and blood of Jesus so we can reinsert him into our lives. Nor is it merely a reminder of some wonderful things that a onetime Jesus did for us a great many Fridays and Sundays ago. It's the real presence, under the signs of bread and wine, of the Jesus who has indwelt all our lives, in all his power, all along. To take another example, the Passover is a sacrament. It's not just a casting back of the communal mind to a liberation that happened once in a distant past, nor is it the celebration of a liberation newly arrived because we have somehow activated it. It is the real presence, at this year's celebration, of the same old liberation that has made us who we have been all along. Witness the words of the Seder ritual in the *Haggadah:*

> In every generation, we should feel as though we ourselves had gone forth from Egypt, as it is written, "And you shall explain to your child on that day, 'It is because of what the Eternal did for me when I, *myself*, went forth from Egypt.'"

And so, by the same token, the church is a sacrament. It's not a Kitchen-Aid mixer that produces the dough of redemption from scratch for people who didn't have cookies before, nor is it just a Kmart aisle sign to remind us that it might be a nice idea to think about making cookies. It's the sign of the *real presence* of the goodies of salvation in everyone, everywhere, from square one. It's God's same old sweets, repackaged.

But enough of the detour: back to Paul. I shall give you just two more instances of his status as part of the identity-defining context of the earliest church.

He started out as a persecutor of the church — as an agent of the historical forces that insured the early church's marginality, and therefore its non-institutional status. A little later on, he was chosen as an Apostle, he says, by none other than Jesus himself on the road to Damascus. Interestingly, this claim was never seriously disputed, even by the Jerusalem church leaders whose cage he constantly rattled: *Jesus* had made him an Apostle, and that was that. (It's an often unnoticed fact of the early church's life that its members didn't just think Jesus was about to come again some other day; they took it for granted that he was also intimately and immediately present in all the affairs of their lives.) In any case, Paul's apostleship gave him such authority in the community that his teaching quickly became perhaps the most definitive of all the contexts in which they found themselves. He was *the* teacher and missionary. He may have written only a pamphlet-sized corpus of work, but all subsequent Christian theology, however massive in volume, is just commentary on it. He became, in a word, *the* Apostle.

And it was in his role as teacher that he became the first to issue a report card on the performance of the early church. I would say that he gave it a C for not resisting the temptations of religion, a B- to warn it against its proclivity to see itself as a new institution, and an F for not being catholic enough by half. But he never ceased to insist that it was capable of straight A's, if only it would listen to him.

But how would I myself grade Paul? He gets an A, I think, for giving a wide berth to the idea that the church was a new *religion*. To the end of his days, it never occurred to him. But he gets only a B+, unfortunately, for his tendency to cave in at times to the blandishments of *institutionalism*. He founded so many churches — and concerned himself so deeply with their ongoing lives — that he got carried away by his fondness for issuing instructions (see 1 Corinthians 7, for example) about what the faithful had to do in order to maintain their membership in those churches. And all that, despite the fact that he was the great granddaddy of the notion that they were a *body* and not a club. Admittedly, when he was writing to churches (such as the one in Rome) that had a fair amount of Jewish ethical probity about them, he could be full of grace and liberation; but when he took on a group like the church in Corinth — whose sexual mores offended his Jewish-uncle soul — he could sound very much like the thunder from Sinai. Finally, though, I give him an A for never once welshing on *catholicity*. From Damascus to his death, he harped on the inclusion of the Gentiles by grace through faith alone as the touchstone of the church's life. And even after his death (if you take the paulinism of Ephesians and Colossians as a faithful extrapolation of Paul), he continued to expand on the catholicity of both the Gospel and the church by raising it to the level of a cosmic mystery.

Altogether, it's a stunning performance for a newcomer. He has to be the top late-bloomer of all time.

5. The Church in the Greco-Roman World

The period from the death of Paul to the Emperor Constantine's issuing of the Edict of Toleration (that is, from 64 to 313 C.E.) saw vast and vibrant changes in the life and form of the church. On the one hand, it became increasingly a Gentile rather than a Jewish phenomenon: its status as the fulfillment of Israel faded into the woodwork of a largely Greek intellectual world. The Jewishness typified by the early Jerusalem church rather quickly evaporated, even on its home soil; and while it continued on as an influence in a few places, most of the churches of the era showed little trace of it. At the same time, the church as a whole began to see itself as an "ecumenical" church, a church of the *oikouménē*, of the then "inhabited world" — a church for the whole *orbis terrarum,* the "circle of lands" around the Mediterranean basin. And with that impressive advance in self-esteem, the church, more seriously than before, was tempted to become both an *institution* and a *religion* in its own right: there's nothing like geographical expansion to encourage a movement to make abstract formulations of its self-identity. On the other hand, the church was to be subject to persecution for almost all of these years. Not continuously: there were times when the secular authorities left it in peace; but there were about ten distinct periods during which it was hounded as a seditious group inimical to the good order of the Empire. This was the period of the martyrs and of the oppressed virgins who became folk heroes of the church's life — and often notable contributors to its religious development.

But it's important, in thinking about this era, to avoid the anachronism of reading back into it later developments of which we are now aware. The church was not yet the institution (or, better said, the successive institutions) it subsequently became. It wasn't yet the church under the undisputed leadership of the bishop of Rome, and it certainly wasn't the church under Constantine, or the Byzantine church, or the medieval Western church — let alone the churches of the Reformation or of the nineteenth and twentieth centuries. If it became an institution, it was by no means an established institution; and if it became a religion, it was saved from at least some of the excesses of religiosity by the fact that it was an illegal religion. There was still a considerable air of risky freedom about it. A shrinking freedom, perhaps, as the rule-making machinery of institutional religion shifted into high gear; but freedom nonetheless.

The life of the earliest church had been marked by a good deal of free experimentation. Acts 2:44-45, for example, depicts a kind of "communism" in which the believers renounced private property, sold their possessions, and distributed the proceeds to all. And 1 Corinthians 9:5 indicates that there were even experiments with new patterns of male-female relationships. (Paul protests there that he too, "just like the rest of the apostles and the Lord's brothers [James of Jerusalem for one] and Cephas [Peter]," has the right to travel around with a "sister wife" in a kind of companionate marriage.)

This liberated and liberating invention of new forms was not unopposed, of course: most of them seem to have gone into the discard, possibly under the steadily growing pressures of conformity to religious standards. But the sense of freedom in Christ that underlay the experimentation continued to be one of the forces that shaped the church of the persecutions. Take the exaltation of martyrdom, for example. The Greco-Roman world was a prudent place. Its sophisticated citizens may have taken the state religion of emperor-worship with several grains of salt, but they went along with it as an insincere gesture of goodwill: they saw it as a harmless bulwark of civil order. They could not understand "these Christians" who insisted on laying down their lives rather than throw a pinch of incense on an altar or surrender a copy of their Scriptures. So too with the virgins and the secular "family values" of the times. Nice Roman girls were supposed to marry the respectable Roman boys their fathers selected for them. Imagine, then, the consternation of those fathers when their daughters insisted on marrying no one but Jesus — when, like Saint Barbara, for instance, they built a tower in the back yard with three windows (one each for the Father, the Son, and the Holy Spirit) and holed themselves up in it. (In passing, isn't it curious that the church nowadays can natter on as if "family values" were part and parcel of its God-given message when Jesus himself took such values cavalierly — and when his virgin brides, at least as society viewed the matter, simply threw them to the wind? As I said, you have to keep a sharp eye out for anachronism.)

But back to a more orderly look at the church from Paul to Constantine. Consider first the church's steady march toward *institutional status*. The *ekklēsía* of the New Testament, as you've seen, came into the Greco-Roman world with a Jewish name that had been filtered to it through the Septuagint translation of the Hebrew Scriptures, where it meant the *assembly* of Israel. But that word *ekklēsía* also had a number of secular meanings, two of which I've already cited for you from the book of Acts: *ekklēsía* as an assembly of people in a specific trade, and *ekklēsía* as a court of law, or at least a session of a court of law. There are, however, still more uses of both *ekklēsía* and *synagōgē* in the common Greek of the time. *Synagōgē* (the term the church *didn't* choose as its name) generally referred to the meetings of various quasi-sacred societies or religious groups, whereas *ekklēsía* was used in connection with political or civic entities. In the "Testament of Epicteta," for example, *synagōgē* refers to the meeting of a society devoted to the worship of heroes; in other sources, *ekklēsía* appears as a reference to such groups as a national assembly or a popular assembly of free citizens. Both words, in short, had institutional overtones; but *ekklēsía* was the more "secular," and had more of them.

In any case, those verbal coincidences were not the only force pressing the church to become an institution. Even at its non-institutional beginning, the church had *leaders* — notably, the Apostles. But any movement that lasts for more than a generation inevitably busies itself with the job of providing for *ongoing leadership:* that is, of turning its original pattern of accepting whatever leaderly cream rose to the top into *offices* to be filled by *officeholders.* You can see this in the later writings of the New Testament itself, all of which were written *after Paul.* In the pastoral epistles (1 Timothy, for example), the titles that were soon to become the names of the various officers of the church (*epískopoi,* "overseers" — and later, "bishops"; *diákonoi,* "deacons"; and *presbýteroi,* "elders," "presbyters" — and eventually, "priests") are already spoken of as if they were definable offices to be filled by suitable candidates. Those offices, admittedly, were still very much in the process of definition (you cannot find the "finished" shape of the church's ministry in the writings of the New Testament, or even at the beginning of this period); but the commitment of the church to an office structure — and the inevitable institutionality that always comes along with such a structure — was firmly in place. And as early as Ignatius of Antioch (who died around 110 C.E.), you have the first appearance of the so-called monarchical episcopate, that is, of the *bishop* as the supreme officeholder of the church — as, in fact, a kind of churchly king.

This was a period of extremely rapid development in the context of a rich secular environment from which the church freely borrowed. Please note once again that this borrowing was not necessarily a bad thing — not "secularism," if you will. It was simply the inevitable working out of the process by which any group, at any time, defines itself: we can think about what we are only in terms of categories and institutions we already have in mind. *Context* — not *just* secular context, of course, but secular context with a vengeance nonetheless — is always in there pitching.

Take the monarchical model of the office of bishop. Jesus didn't act, or look like a king. Nor did Peter or James of Jerusalem (though he probably had a talent for it). Nor did Paul, though he could be imperious. So where did the supremacy of bishops come from? From the context. From, in this instance, the *kingly model* that stood before the church's eyes in the person of the Roman emperor. There were at least three aspects of that royal model that could handily serve the church as it shaped its life — and, in particular, its "official" life: the king as *warrior,* the king as *administrator,* and the king as *shepherd.* The *warrior* role was easily taken over as a model of episcopacy. Externally, the young church found itself beset by persecutors who quite naturally took as their targets its most visible members, namely, the bishops. (Ignatius, for example, ended his career in martrydom.) Valiance on behalf of the church, therefore, came to be seen as one of the obligations of those in positions of leadership, even if it resulted in the death of the leader. And internally, that same valiance was exercised with relish (and with a somewhat better chance of survival) by the episcopate. The church was not so young that it hadn't experienced theological dissension in the ranks. Accordingly, the bishops began to see themselves as the first line of defense against heresy — and soon enough as the established agency for the authentic expression of the apostolic witness of the church.

The *administrative* role of the king was likewise attractive to the church and its bishops. Paul had indeed been something of an administrator, but he moved so often that he never got around to institutionalizing his exercise of the role. As the church settled down in the cities of the Greco-Roman world, however, more stable patterns of administration began to appear. This all took time, of course, and did not come to full flower until after Constantine. But throughout the second and third centuries, even in the times of persecution, the lines of an administrative flow-chart emerged more and more clearly. Bishops presided at the Eucharist. Bishops ordained other ministers. Bishops issued letters of instruction to their flock. And it was bishops who sat in council with other bishops when the church's disputes had to be settled.

But it was the image of the king as *shepherd* that really made all those businesslike aspects of the royal model acceptable to the church. It may surprise you that "shepherd of his people" was one of the titles of an ancient king, but it was definitely a function of royalty as then conceived. To some degree, no doubt, it stemmed from the talent for public relations that comes naturally to all political figures: any image that says "Good Guy" is a good image to latch on to. But it was taken with sufficient seriousness, in enough times and instances, not only for the note of pastoral concern to take up residence in the secular concept of kingship but for that particular aspect of the royal model to seem appropriate to a church that already thought of itself as the body of Christ, the Good Shepherd.

Two other models of Greco-Roman institutional life, and we can move on. The Romans had a Latin word for what the secular Greek of the time occasionally referred to as *synagōgé,* and that word was *collegium.* Without going into it in any depth, I would describe the *collegium* as a voluntary association of persons devoted to some specific end or activity — rather like what we would call a lodge or a benevolent society. If you joined one and fulfilled your obligations, you enjoyed whatever privileges came with membership while you lived and usually, when you died, got a decent burial in the bargain. In any case, the *collegia* of those times were sufficiently like the church in their voluntary, obligational, and mortuary aspects for the church to take them as something of a model for its self-identification: it had all of those aspects, plus officers and functionaries, and so could easily see itself as a similar institution.

The other and more important model was the Roman *familia.* The noble family household of this period was not confined to parents and children. It was a thoroughly extended proposition, consisting of wife, children, grandparents, assorted hangers-on related by blood, tutors and high-ranking servants who were frequently slaves, and plenty of other slaves to do the menial work — all under the hopefully benevolent rule of the male head of the household, the *paterfamilias.* Needless to say, this particular institutional model suited the church to a T. It had long thought of itself in familial terms (witness its early habit of calling itself "the brethren"). It was not just a voluntary society but the result of forces beyond the will of the individual members: in the case of the Roman *familia,* the household was based on blood relationship and/or involuntary servitude, and in the case of the church, on divine election, not merely human choice — and in both it was meant to be a household that nurtured and provided for its members. But above all, the role of *paterfamilias* was eminently comfortable to the bishops as they increasingly fastened their grip on the church's life. As they did with the role of king, they found the combination of authoritative rule and benevolent concern the very thing they were looking for.

And so, as a result of borrowing from all these models, the church in short order became an institution. But if there was much that was either good or harmless in this development, there was still a very large aspect of it that introduced a danger into the church's life. By now, its existence over a period of time as *the same entity* that had gotten rolling at Pentecost quite naturally led it to pattern itself after other institutions that endured despite the departure of some of their human components. But when it chose such institutional models, it chose entities that were seriously less than human — that were, for all the world, indistinguishable from *angels*. For institutions are precisely angelic. Corporations, kingships, courts, voluntary societies, and even families are not simply human beings doing x, y, or z; they are great, ethereal egos in their own right who are not only more important than the people under their patronage but who can also lead those who fall under their sway to do sometimes quite inhuman, not to mention un-Christian, things.

One down-home, modern illustration. Think of the pastor of a church caught in some sin: let's make it adultery, just to be sure your attention doesn't wander. And think of the reaction of the Official Board of that church to the gentleman's dereliction. As merely human beings who profess to follow Jesus as forgiven sinners themselves, they could easily forgive him and leave him in place as their pastor. It's possible that each of them may have pardoned him for being a known drunk, backbiter, money-grubber, or bore; there is therefore no Christian reason for them not to pardon his now-public roll in the hay. But as the *Official Board of First Steeple Church* they have no such option, for the simple reason that the Board is an angel and can never forgive anybody. They will convince themselves that the honor, or the dignity, or the reputation of First Steeple

— plus their responsibility as underlings of the angel of First Steeple
— would make it quite impossible for them to do any such ir-
responsible thing.

To be sure, there is such a thing as predatory behavior, and it
can indeed do dreadful things to its victims. But the church has to
find other ways of protecting the innocent than simply running
sinners off the ecclesiastical farm. The hardest thing to teach a
two-year-old is that a long stick has two ends. A child with a six-foot
bamboo pole may think she's only pushing a ball along the rug with
the short end; but meanwhile, the long end is knocking her mother's
Limoges off the mantelpiece. The worst thing about the church's
current preoccupation with sexual offenses is that however "right"
it may be in the short term to move clergy out because of them,
the sad result is that the crockery of the Gospel of forgiveness gets
swept off the church's shelf by the long-term obsession with good
behavior. The world has long been convinced that the church's main
business is sin prevention, and that the salvation we proclaim is a
matter of getting people to straighten up and fly right. We ought
to think two-hundred-times twice before we risk throwing salvation
by grace alone into the angelic trash can any more than we already
have.

All across the institutional board, the same angelic tyranny
prevails. Children are disinherited by the angel of the Family, presi-
dents are under judgment by the angel of the Presidency, romantic
lovers who stray are condemned by the angel of Romance — and
so on and on, into the dark night of angelic institutional perfection
that makes mincemeat of flesh and blood. And nowhere is that night
darker or more dangerous than in the institutional church. Nowhere
is it more destructive of the people and purposes for which the
institution supposedly exists. Our two-thousand-year love affair with
excommunication — with the expulsion of sinners, heretics, and
other troublemakers — has been a disaster for the Good News of
free grace. I think the real reason why God saved the world by
becoming human rather than sending some angel to do the job was
that, as incarnate in our flesh, he could simply lay down his life for
sinners, whereas any angel he might have sent, precisely because it

couldn't lay down its life for a soul, would never have shut up on the subject of sin.

But enough of the church as institution. Meanwhile, back at the Greco-Roman ranch, the church was just as busy becoming a *religion*. As you know, the notion of *eusébeia,* meaning "piety" or "godliness," had gotten a foothold in the later writings of the New Testament; so also, to a more modest degree, had the notion of *thrēskeía,* meaning "worship" or "religion" as such. Interestingly, that was not so from the start. In the early chapters of Acts, both words are used to *contrast* what the church really considered itself to be (namely, not a religion) with what other people thought about it: *eusébeia,* to deny that the Apostles had any *piety* of their own; and *thrēskeía,* to refer to the strictness of Paul's *religion* as a Pharisee. But in 1 Timothy, for example, *eusébeia* is put forth as a *praiseworthy characteristic* of church membership. Try these references on for size: "that we may lead a quiet and peaceable life in all *godliness* and dignity" (1 Tim. 2:2); "without any doubt, the mystery of our *religion* is great" (1 Tim. 3:16); "train yourself in *godliness*" (1 Tim. 4:7). And in James, *thrēskeía* is held up for admiration: "*religion* that is pure and undefiled before God, the Father, is this: to care for orphans and widows in their distress, and to keep oneself unstained from the world" (Jas. 1:26).

Religion, as it is usually put forth, has three characteristics: *creed, cult,* and *conduct. Creed* stands for the propositional "faith-content" of what the believers hold to be true; *cult,* for the religious practices they employ; and *conduct,* for the moral demands of their religion. How did the church in the Greco-Roman world score in these categories?

As far as *creed* was concerned, the church had already developed a brief confession of faith — namely, the Apostles' Creed — which it referred to in Greek as a *sýmbolon,* or "roundup" of what candidates for baptism were required to believe. Minimal though that creed was, however, it was enough to get Christians thinking of their faith in Jesus as a matter of *propositions.* Furthermore, theological *orthodoxy* became a matter of growing concern during this period. In the writings of the so-called Apostolic Fathers (late first century through the second century), the stigmatization of heresy had clearly begun. Ignatius of Antioch, for example, inveighed against the Docetic heresy (the assertion that Christ's humanity was only an appearance, not a reality). All in all, the creedal aspect of the church as a *religion* was growing more and more impressive.

On the subject of *cult,* the church had long since taken the less-than-cultic act of recalling Jesus' death as a common criminal by breaking bread and drinking wine and made it the central act of its worship. Soon enough, it would also take the word "mystery" *(mystḗrion)* — by which it had originally referred either to the work of God manifested in Jesus himself or to the church as the body of Christ — and make it the name of that liturgical act. The Eucharist became "the holy *mysteries*" — for which the Latin equivalent was the word *sacramentum,* "sacrament." *Sacramentum* originally referred to a military oath of allegiance, and then to the emblems on which the oath was taken; it was not, in Roman usage, a particularly religious word. But *mystḗrion* was part and parcel of the stock phraseology of a host of Greek religions, and thus tended to carry the freight of its religiosity right into the life of the church. In any case, the developing *liturgy* of the church is occasionally portrayed in this period. In the *Dídachē,* for example ("The Teaching of the Twelve Apostles," included in the "Apostolic Fathers"), there is a description of an (admittedly idiosyncratic) Eucharist as it was celebrated at the time. Religion as cult was growing right along with religion as creed in the life of the church.

But it was in the matter of *conduct* that religion got its strongest foothold in the life of the church before Constantine. There is nothing intrinsically contrary to the church's mission, of course, in the suggestion that an upright life might be a good thing for Christians to attempt. But when that suggestion reaches the point at which it becomes a test of membership in the church, it comes smack up against a radical peculiarity of the Gospel: *Jesus was not a teacher of ethics.* The Sermon on the Mount, for instance, is not a string of sensible lessons in morality: it's a paradoxical presentation, in the *form* of ethical advice, of recipes for getting yourself creamed. And the radical Gospel of grace and forgiveness that is the church's deepest message isn't ethics, either. It's an outrageously unethical offer not to count anybody's sins at all, because the Lamb of God simply stopped counting when he drew everybody to himself on the cross. At its root, therefore, the Gospel is immoral, not moral: it lets scoundrels in free for nothing.

However, once the church started down the road of setting up ethical behavior as a standard for membership, it quickly became a religion much like other religions. And that descent (not only from the Gospel but from the less-than-religious character of the earliest church) was accelerated in this period by the fact that the church, quite rightly and inevitably, felt it had to take a stand against the religions (from emperor-worship to mystery cults) that surrounded it in the Greco-Roman world. Unfortunately, though, that stand had troublesome consequences. You cannot wrestle with a tar baby without getting tar on yourself. And, by the same token, you cannot stigmatize the falsity of other religions without being fatally tempted to see yourself as the true religion — and thus ending up as simply one more *religion*. Which is exactly what the church did. It picked up the ball of *eusébeia-thrēskeía* that had been fumbled in the later New Testament and ran with it toward the wrong goal line.

This is not to say that the church went straight downhill at this point. In the writings of the Apostolic Fathers, there are some signs of resistance to this religionizing tendency. In "The Shepherd of Hermas," for example, there is an insistence that post-baptismal sin is *not* unforgivable — which implies, of course, that some people took the religious view that it was. And there is much else, especially in the writing of Clement of Rome, that is as pauline as Paul himself on the subject of religion. (First Clement, in fact, was regarded as Scripture by some Christians until the fourth century.) But on balance, the drive toward the church as a *religious institution* — as the agency of a *Christian religion* — went on throughout the period.

The trouble with all of that can be simply put. Religion, to say it again, is always a *transaction* — always something that people do for God in order to get God to do something for them. But since the Gospel is the proclamation that God has once and for all done everything that needs doing, Christianity as a religion is always at odds with the Gospel. This is a point that applies not only to the church in the Greco-Roman world but to all succeeding periods of the church's life, including our own. In fact, with the revival of religion at the present time (and of fundamentalist religion at that), I would say it's one of the biggest problems we now have.

But to round out the discussion of the period we're currently dealing with: how did the church at this juncture fare on the subject of *catholicity?* Well, *mezza-mezza.* On the one hand, it was in this period that the word *catholic* itself came into fashion (in the New Testament it appears only once, and then not in the sense it later came to have). The church, now extended to many places and peoples — and extended backward in time to all the previous periods of its existence — needed a word that would bolster its conviction that, through all those manifestations, it was still the same church, holding the same faith. And the word *katholikē* filled the bill. In its etymological sense, it meant "according to the whole"; but practically, it was used to mean "in universal agreement" regardless of time or place. It was not a bad start.

On the other hand, the growing *religiosity* of the church was pushing the all-important universality of the Gospel into the shade. As the *true religion,* it inevitably came to see itself as the religion of *some* rather than as the sacrament of a truth about *all.* Requirements for membership (and hence the possibility of loss of membership) loomed larger and larger in the church's imagination. We had begun our progress toward the point at which we now stand (and have stood for some five hundred years): the point at which, in common usage, the phrase "the Catholic Church" now refers to a particular religious institution to which not even all Christians belong. Admittedly, the church at this time was saved from some of the most catholicity-threatening features of its burgeoning status as a religious institution by the fact that it was an *illegal* religion. It might tie itself up in knots with religious requirements, but it had no effective power to put the arm on anybody else. And while the persecutions were not constant throughout the era, they were frequent enough and painful enough to suggest that running everybody's religious life might not have to be thought of as the church's main job. But with Constantine just below the horizon of the future, those shaky bulwarks of catholicity were scheduled for demolition.

Before we turn the page to the next period, however, I want to conclude this chapter with a few remarks on the loss of catholicity that the church of the late first to third centuries incurred when, as a *new religion,* it set out on the course of ignoring its roots in Judaism — and thus planted the seeds of subsequent anti-Semitism.

True enough, the church in the city of Rome at the beginning of this period represented a rather Jewish Christianity — much as it had earlier when Paul, comfortable with the Jewishness of his audience for the epistle to the Romans, had found it possible to write such a calm and reasonable treatise. And the Jewishness of that church even continued into the time of the Apostolic Fathers: both Hermas and Second Clement attest to it. But in the increasingly Gentile church at large, its origin as Israel in fulfillment, *not as Israel superseded,* slipped more and more to the back of the ecclesiastical mind. The church had become a Greco-Roman phenomenon: the "Greek drift" of Christianity away from Judaism had begun in earnest. Once again, the church's lack of secular power to implement its growing anti-Semitism seems to have kept it from doing its worst with regard to the Jews. But the philosophical underpinnings of the eventual tragedy were already in place.

A case in point was Marcion, a second-century son of a bishop whom the wider church had the good grace to label as a heretic. Marcion had a mind rife with odd speculations, and he eventually emerged as an influential teacher in Rome. His most notable doctrine, perhaps, was that there were actually two Gods: one, the Creator and Judge, and the other, the God revealed in Jesus. Accordingly, he came to the obvious conclusion that it was the inferior Creator-God who was responsible for the Hebrew Scriptures — and so went straight on to repudiate the whole of those Scriptures. But Marcion wasn't all bad: he was very much in favor of Paul, even claiming, in his typically extravagant fashion, that Paul was the only Apostle. But he is an instance of how far the Gentile mind could get from the Judaism in which the church had once found its definition of itself.

To sum up this chapter, then: the church in the period before Constantine had become a religion as well as an institution; and it had both invented, and begun to compromise, the notion of catholicity. The "angels" were already vying for control over its mind — and just around the corner of history stood the largest and longest-running angel of all: the Christendom model of the church that would be ushered in by Constantine.

6. The Christendom Model of the Church

So far, I've given you two models of the church since the day of Pentecost: the *Judaism model,* which, as it had been embodied by the early church, was pretty much in collapse by the end of the first century C.E.; and the *Christian religious institution model* that replaced it almost everywhere in the second and third centuries. But as we head into the fourth century, we come to the beginnings of something new for the still young church. Having started out as a movement which, precisely because of the marginality of its Jewishness, had little or no influence on the established secular order of the time — and having spent the rest of its first three hundred years as a similarly marginal Christian church — it now became, first, a legal religion; next, the religion of the emperor; and, by the end of the fourth century, the established religion of the Empire itself, east and west. The notion of a Christian *society,* of church and state hand in glove, had made its appearance for the first time. *Christendom* had finally been invented.

This marriage of religion and politics, of course, was not completely new: as we've seen, the people of Israel had come up with something very like it in the period of the Monarchy-Temple model. As a matter of fact, it was precisely that Hebraic model which the medieval and Reformation versions of Christendom picked up as a God-given parallel to their ecclesiastical and political situation. Nor was the state-church model, any more than the others we've already seen, a complete disaster. A church proclaiming the incarnation of God in human flesh could quite rightly, once it got the political opportunity, concern itself with secular human affairs. I would even go so far as to say that it was the very rightness of that concern — and of the concomitant notion of a society entirely permeated by Christian values — that was the source of both the beauty and the longevity of the Christendom model. Hands down, it held the endurance record for Christian models of the people of God. In the Old Testament period, the *Exodus* model had lasted two hundred fifty years, the *monarchical* model, four hundred plus, and the *postexilic* model less than five hundred (though from the point of view of Judaism itself, it wins the game overall at nearly two thousand five hundred years). And in the period of the New Testament and beyond, the *Jerusalem church* model lasted less than a hundred years and the marginal *Greco-Roman* model only three hundred. But so great were the charms — and, of course, the political timing — of the *Christendom* model that it endured for fifteen hundred years, all the way into the nineteenth century. True enough, it was on its last legs from the sixteenth century onward. Still, any model that can keep up a swan song for that long has got to be a super-model.

But not to get ahead of the story: there's a lot to cover in this chapter, and I want to give you the highlights as succinctly as possible — beginning, naturally, with the Emperor Constantine.

Flavius Valerius Aurelius Constantinus, Constantine the First — and the Great, and even (for the Orthodox churches of the East) the Saint — was the first Roman emperor acknowledged to have become a Christian. He was born in the 280s and was probably on hand and in politics (his family's trade) for the last of the persecutions under the Emperor Diocletian in 303. By this time, the administration of the Roman Empire was already divided into western and eastern branches — Constantine's father Constantius having been named as Augustus of the west in 305 and Galerius as Augustus of the east some time before that. Though Constantine's actual assignment was in the east, he managed to thwart Galerius' wishes and join his father in Gaul and, later, Britain. And when his father died at York in 306, the troops proclaimed the young Constantine himself Augustus.

Not satisfied with being Caesar in the boondocks, however, he invaded Italy and, having caused a Christian monogram to be painted on his soldiers' shields, finally defeated the local opposition at the battle of the Milvian bridge in 312. Whether he considered himself a Christian at this time is hard to tell — he certainly wasn't baptized until he was on his deathbed in 337. But what is certain is that his Edict of Toleration, making Christianity a legal religion, was issued in 313 — and that from then on he considered himself the chosen instrument of the "Highest Divinity" (which for him meant the God of the Christians). On balance, though, he seems at this time to have viewed the Christian God more as a kind of "God paramount" over the pagan gods than as the only true God. His excursions into religious matters can perhaps best be seen as exercises of the traditional duty of the emperor to maintain the *pax deorum,* the "peace of the gods." Only later did he take active measures to oppose paganism.

Constantine seems to have been a skillful general, a successful if capricious politician, and a middling theologian who quickly maneuvered himself into a position of extensive meddling in — no, that's too weak a word: into the outright supervision of church affairs. On the military-political front, he moved adroitly to put down his opponents and to rebuild the city of Byzantium; and in 330, he formally rededicated the city, renaming it, in the style of the political animal he was, Constantinople. But even before that, realizing that the church in the east was larger and more influential — and, in particular, more fractious — than the church in the west, he set himself to the task of resolving its controversies. Most notably, he undertook to resolve the dispute (between Alexander, bishop of Alexandria, and Arius, one of his priests) over whether Christ was truly God or just a kind of junior God. He called an ecumenical council at Nicea in 325 and succeeded in getting it to produce a creed that declared Christ to be "of one substance *(homooúsios)* with the Father." The matter was not finally settled until 451, at the Council of Chalcedon; but the pattern of imperial management of church affairs was well entrenched by the time Constantine died. He supported Athanasius, the successor of Alexander, as the orthodox champion for a while; but in his desire to get Arius back in the fold, he finally called another council at Tyre in 335, had Athanasius condemned, and banished him to Gaul.

How well Constantine understood the theological points at issue is a good question. Principally, his goal as far as the church was concerned was to get it to settle its hash for the sake of the good order of the Empire. And while he later issued an edict urging all his subjects to become Christians (a policy that resulted in the usual large number of conversions based on self-interest), he continued to tolerate paganism for some time. Eventually, though, he moved against it, destroying temples and confiscating their treasures. By the time he died, the Empire had for most intents and purposes become Christendom. And except for the brief (361-363) reign of Julian the Apostate (even his title is a tribute to the new model), that model's seemingly indestructible union of church and state continued almost to our own time. (In fact, the present-day "religious right" seems to think that the marriage is, or at least should be, still going strong.)

This brings us to the subject of the church and *power* — specifically, of what I choose to refer to as *left-handed* rather than right-handed power. Right-handed power is the ordinary kind of force by means of which we accomplish almost everything in the world: direct force, aimed at producing a direct effect. I squeeze the toothpaste from the tube, turn on the water faucet, raise the toothbrush to my mouth, and clean my teeth by right-handed power, even if I use my left hand to do it. Water is boiled, cathedrals are built, taxes are collected, wars are fought, and love is made — all by right-handed power: by using sufficient energy, on suitable material, to produce the desired result. In terms of the sheer number of effects that occur in the physical world, perhaps 99.99999 percent of them are caused by just that kind of power.

But as early as the story of Noah, God renounced that kind of power. After strong-arming the world with the Flood, he put up the Rainbow and swore he'd never do anything like that again. Because there is one effect that cannot be the result of a direct application of force, and that is *the maintenance of a relationship between free persons.* If my child chooses not to cooperate with me, if my wife chooses not to live with me, there is no right-handed power on earth that can make them toe the line of relationship I have chosen to draw in the sand. I can dock my son's allowance, for example, or chain him to a radiator; or in anger at my wife, I can punch holes in the Sheetrock or beat her senseless with a shovel. In short, I can use any force that comes to hand or mind, and yet I cannot cause either of them, at the core of their being, to stop their wrongs and conform to my right. The only power I have by which to do that is *left-handed power* — which for all practical purposes will be indistinguishable from weakness on my part. It is the power of my patience with them, of my letting their wrongs be — even if that costs me my rightness or my life — so that they, for whose reconciliation I long, may live for a better day of their own choosing.

My point here is twofold. The power of God that saves the world was revealed in Jesus as left-handed power; and therefore any power that the church may use in its God-given role as the sacrament of Jesus must also be left-handed. Despite the fact that God's Old Testament forays into the thicket of fallen human nature were decidedly right-handed (plagues, mighty acts, stretched-out-arm exercises, and thunderous threats) — and despite Jesus' occasional use of similar tactics in the Gospels — the final act by which God reconciles the world to himself consists of his simply dropping dead on the cross and shutting up on the subject of sin. He declares the whole power game won by losing, and he invites the world just to believe that absurd proposition.

Accordingly, for as long as the church is marginal with regard to the secular exercise of power, it has at least a leg up on its mission to be the sacrament of left-handed power. But when it jumps into the sack with the state, it is mightily tempted to turn itself into just one more presence of the same old bare-knuckled force that never did and never can resist the temptation to put the arm on sinners. The "conversion" of Europe by the baptism of whole tribes at spear point was not one of the great sacramental moments of the Dark Ages. That the church can do (and has done) a great many good and gorgeous things with the right-handed power it acquired by marrying the state is of course one of the glories of its history. But the final truth about the disaster of its involvement with Caesar is that those achievements do not represent the heart of its God-given mission. We are not sent to build cathedrals, however beautiful, or to run parish fairs, however productive of contributions to the institutional budget. We are sent to proclaim the foolishness of God that is wiser than human beings and the weakness of God that is stronger than human beings (1 Cor. 1:25) — all of which is a scandal to the Jew in us and idiocy to the Greek. Marginality, in short, leaves the church free, if it is faithful, to cherish its absurdity; establishment just makes it fall in love all over again with the irrelevant respectability of the world's wisdom and power.

Furthermore, since the state is inevitably both perishable in time and parochial in place, it makes a poor model for a church that is supposed to be catholic with regard to both: the church finds itself continually egged into faking its catholicity. Instead of embracing its timeless absurdity, it latches onto the transitory plausibility of the model it has fallen in love with and defends that model's limited boundaries as if they were the full extent of what it means to be "catholic." And then it consigns everybody else — the rest of the ragtag, catholic mass of humanity for whom Jesus died — either to insignificance or to excommunication. It forgets, for example, that it was ever Jewish; or it remembers those of other religions only as "souls benighted." Or, instead of pursuing its catholic mission to proclaim Jesus' already-accomplished *finding* of all people in all places, it settles down in the places it happens to occupy by the power of the state and writes off the infidels as *lost:* it puts the Jews into ghettos and rides the other recalcitrants out of town on a rail, or in a box. And then, to cap the climax, it refers to the states in which all this gleeful exclusion takes place as "catholic countries." In the end, catholic just ain't catholic anymore.

Moving very quickly now through the millennium-and-a-half of the Christendom model: it was as good as it was bad as it was dreadful. The Byzantine church of the East had its beauties, and it produced churches, saints, theologians, missionaries, and ordinary

Christians of extraordinary proportions — and a great deal of wealth in the bargain. Likewise, the Latin church of the West became the bulwark of civilization after the fall of Rome and went on to foster the glories of the medieval synthesis: the monasteries, the cities, the cathedrals, the guilds — the flowering, if you will, of all the good things that can be done by right-handed power at its best. But the church, both East and West, also went on to produce (however pervasive it may have been) an essentially *closed* society — for the simple reason that it was by now inseparable from an institutional order that necessarily had to distinguish citizens from outlaws. And the device it used was simple. Citizenship in western medieval Europe (through the feudal period, through the High Middle Ages, and on into the time of the advent of nation-states) was a matter of baptism: if you were a Christian, you were in; if not, not. *Christendom,* as an amalgam of church and state, became almost synonymous with the civil order, and the mission of the church shrank to maintaining the parameters of a temporal and spatial phenomenon. The church, in a word, became a chaplaincy.

Admittedly, for as long as the quasi-historical myth of the Holy Roman Empire remained a (somewhat) relevant way of thinking about the lightly linked-up societies of western Europe, the Christendom model provided the church with both a philosophical and a practical sense of unity — and above all with a sense of power. Increasingly, the church gained the upper hand over the ramshackle state of the time. In 1077, for example, Pope Gregory VII kept the Emperor Henry IV waiting three days in the snow at Canossa before inviting him in and un-excommunicating him. And until the triumph of Islam in the East, the Caesaro-papism of the Byzantine church built up much the same kind of ecclesiastical muscle there. But with the next turn of the historical screw — with the flowering of the nation-states in the West and the secular anarchy of Greek Christianity in the East — the stage was set, particularly in the Latin part of Christendom, for the beginning of the end of the model. Which brings us nicely — in this hop, skip, and jump survey (remember: this book is not a history but an argument *from* history) — to the era of the Reformation.

Once again, it is the *historical context* of the church — specifically, the context of the late-medieval version of the Christendom model — that becomes one of the principal factors in the ongoing development (or denouement) of the church's self-identity. What happened to the medieval model of the church during the Reformation was, despite the Reformers' good intentions, a disaster. By the very fact that their reforming was done directly after the theological and political turmoil of the fourteenth and fifteenth centuries — and, in particular, because it was done under the aegis of the *emerging nation-states* of the West — they insured that the first fatal cracks would begin to appear in the foundations of Christendom.

The Reformation began as a movement seeking to undo the abuses of the late-medieval period as they had been inherited by the sixteenth-century Latin church. Notably (from the point of view of my argument), it continued to wrestle — as had such predecessors as the Lollards, the Hussites, and the Conciliar Movement of the century before — with the religious and institutional problems that the Christendom model had foisted on the church. Luther, for example, started out as an Augustinian monk who was, among many other things, an heir of earlier reformers who had insisted on such radical notions as vernacular translations of the Scriptures, communion in both kinds, the abandonment of clerical celibacy, the poverty of the clergy, and the expropriation of church property. At the beginning of his career, he even entertained the conservative reformist hope that a general council might be called which would accomplish those ends. There had been and there were, of course, wild-eyed left-wingers who were more than willing to go into schism. But the early Luther was not one of them.

Events, however, caught up with him. Having been raised in the late-medieval atmosphere of guilt, and in fear of judgment by the punishing severity of God, he found that the transactions which the church (as, by now, the principal *agency* of salvation) offered him for the removal of those fears simply did nothing for him. The *justice* of God — and the human *righteousness* required to please a God who would consign the whole human race to damnation unless it straightened up and submitted to the church's ministrations —

continued to haunt him. It was only after long study of Paul (and, in particular, of the epistle to the Romans) that he broke his way through to the finally liberating understanding that righteousness was not something he had to work up on his own but a gift that God gave him by free grace in Christ — a gift to be received *by faith alone,* without a single work of any kind required.

But this liberation had more than personal and theological consequences; it had political ones as well. You cannot diminish the power with which an institution dominates its members by fear without encouraging those who resent that dominance — those further down the institutional ladder — to liberate themselves from whatever other constraints they may feel oppressed by. As early as the end of the 1300s, under the influence of Lollardy, for example, peasants' revolts against landowners had begun in Europe. And by the year 1524, a similar revolt against the propertied classes (and, to a degree, against the propertied church as well) was underway in Germany. But the nobility of Germany (by the very fact that the Christendom model had for so long made them dependent on the church for the justification of their status, and vice versa) were not about to sit still for such a threat. The nobility, however, also had reasons to support Luther: while they cherished the church as a bulwark of civil order, they were also increasingly disenchanted with the financial exactions and general meddling of the papal establishment. But precisely because Luther was being courted by both parties, he had a decision to make.

Logically and theologically, perhaps, he should have sided with the peasants; but in fact he came down squarely on the side of the nobility. Why? Well, I would put it this way: while he was able to rid himself of the theological aspects of the Christendom model that plagued him (guilt, fear, condemnation, salvation as an ecclesiastical transaction), he was not able to break free of the political notion that the union of church and state was of divine origin. In any case, in 1523 he had already written the treatise "Of Earthly Government," in which he asserted the duty of civil obedience and the sinfulness of rebellion against lawful authority; and by 1525 he had graduated to the tirade "Against the Murdering, Thieving Hordes of Peasants." The established state churches of Lutheranism were only a few miles down the road.

To give another example, much the same kind of thing happened in England. Henry VIII started out as a loyal son of the Western church. (In fact, the title "Defender of the Faith" that still graces the British monarch was first given to the young Henry as a reward for a manifesto he wrote against Luther.) But once again the historical context called the shots. Henry's father, Henry VII, had been the first king of what was fast becoming the English nation-state. The Wars of the Roses between the houses of Lancaster and York for supremacy over England had only just ceased at the end of the fifteenth century. Henry, therefore, not having a legitimate male heir (and not wanting to risk a new civil war over the succession to his throne), decided to divorce the Spanish princess, Catherine of Aragon, who had failed to bear him a son, and to marry Anne Boleyn, of whose son-producing talents he was more confident. The Pope, under the watchful eye and thumb of the Spanish monarchy, was no help. In fact, he dallied so long over Henry's request for an annulment that Henry, at the end of his patience, had Parliament declare *him* the head of the church in England — and then had his own Archbishop of Canterbury do the favor for him.

If such state-church hanky-panky sounds terribly political to us now, it was. But the important thing to note is that, as a result of centuries of acquiescence in the Christendom model of the church — and of the happy chance to retool for a new version of that model — it simply seemed like an appropriate way out of a not inconsiderable difficulty. After all, church and state had been yoked for a millennium. Not only that, but the genuinely powerful states which once were the church's partners (Rome, Byzantium) had long since gone whistling down the wind. And the version of Christendom that had replaced them was no great shakes: it was a loosely linked-up feudal arrangement presided over by an evanescent Holy Roman Empire that was mostly under the pope's heel. So why shouldn't the church, now that there were states with a bark to them rising all over Europe, just go with the flow of history and refit the Christendom model for an appointment with the glory of its yesteryears?

To say again something I noted at the outset: the only people available to run the Reformation had been born and raised as late medievalists. That coincidence served them both well and badly: where they recognized a medieval abuse, they righted it; but where they didn't, they perpetuated it. Take the theological arena, for example. When they saw that the medieval system of salvation by works violated the Gospel of salvation by grace through faith alone, they promptly championed grace and excoriated works. But on the other hand, when they failed to recognize that the medieval preoccupation with the punishment of sinners was a Trojan horse filled with the forces of works-righteousness, they made no such root-and-branch effort to get rid of it. Damnation, in the popular mind, remained a much more vivid fate than salvation. The same thing was true in the political arena. The Reformers may have made a host of relatively minor changes in matters such as whether priests could marry, or who had the right to appoint bishops and prescribe forms of worship; but when it came to questioning the right of the state to dictate and enforce the answers to such posers, they never saw anything to question. They never (except for extreme groups, such as the Anabaptists and assorted other heirs of the late-medieval rabble-rousers) seriously doubted the applicability of the Christendom model to their own time.

And so it was that they inadvertently set in motion the very thing that would eventually destroy it. As the sixteenth century progressed, *they produced mini-Christendoms all over Europe,* thus compartmentalizing Europe into a mare's nest of religious enclaves. Luther's tactical giveaway to the nobility (*cuius regio, eius religio* — only the king has freedom of religion) carried the day. The assumption was that if a state religion was good enough for David, Solomon, Constantine, and Company, it was more than good enough for the Reformers. They never asked whether the Christendom model had really done the church all the favors it claimed; instead, they went right on assuming that despite its recent muddying under the management of the bishop of Rome, a trip through the reforming car wash would make it as good as new. They felt quite happy in the conviction that what had once been would now go on forever.

But it would not. In fact, their invention of mini-Christen-doms was the beginning of the death rattle of Christendom itself. You cannot farm out a flawed vision of catholicity to a bunch of branch offices without coming up with something less catholic still. The church now became the *churches* of the Reformation. Even the Roman Church, which (as did the others, according to their ability) clung to the notion that it was the only true church, was in reality just another Reformation church after the Council of Trent. Roman Catholicism, as we now think of it, was not a medieval phenome-non. In the Middle Ages, Rome presided over a (mostly) united Christian church that included (almost) everybody. But when it stepped into the free-for-all of reformed religions with its Creed of Pius the Fifth, it inevitably became, despite its ongoing claim to be *the* church, simply *one of the churches*. Worse yet, all of those churches, contrary to Christianity's original status as *no religion at all*, ended up even more religious than before. Religion may have been one of the diseases of the church almost from the start; but, despite the ministrations of the Reformers, it came out of their course of treatment in a more virulent form than ever.

Part of this continuing infection was the church's newfound enthusiasm for the *creedal* aspect of religion. As you've already seen, *confessions of faith* — exhaustive (and exhausting) definitions of what had to be believed or anathematized — were produced right and left. Practically speaking, subscription to a confession replaced the simple baptismal symbol as the *sine qua non* of church membership, and off we went down the road at the end of which Protestantism turned into the heap of splinters it now is. But even the exponential splintering did not dampen the zeal with which the churches ex-communicated not only their fractious members but each other as well. It had been bad enough that the churches of East and West had broken their unity in the eleventh century; but that was next to nothing compared to the shipwreck of catholicity in the aftermath of the Reformation.

God, however, refused to sit still for it. He doesn't just show off by riding the bicycle of history home no-hands; for the fun of it, apparently, he gets off every now and then and practices throwing sinker pitches at the church. You've seen it once already, when he pitched out the Monarchy-Temple model by throwing the Babylonian Captivity at it. And you are about to see it again — this time, in the seventeenth century.

As you know, the period of the Reformation coincided with the age of exploration and the growth of international trade that quickly followed it. You might think that the mini-Christendom model would have impeded trade: the restrictive combination of state churches and divisive confessions of faith should have thrown a large, wet blanket over commercial activity. It's risky business to make deals with people your government's religion would just as soon see dead, gone, or both. But business, being its mercantile self, makes it its business to find a way. If the entrepreneurs of the seventeenth century could not trade freely on their home turf with Christians of other persuasions, they would find someplace else where they could. And as I've pointed out, that place was waiting for them in the Low Countries — courtesy, mainly, of the Dutch. Not that the Dutch were any less given to the confessional enthusiasms of the age than their counterparts elsewhere: they held their own nicely in that department. But they were also businessmen with considerable international holdings, and they were not as enthusiastic as some theological types about letting religion stand in the way of getting and gaining. It was in the Netherlands, therefore, that the opposing religionists who couldn't make a buck off each other at home met to do just that.

I know. I have mentioned all this — plus the concomitant philosophical development of the notion of individual human rights — in the overview I gave you at the beginning of this book; but this is where it comes in as part of my argument. I won't belabor it any further in this chapter, except to say that once mercantilism and philosophy had shot the Reformation version of the Christendom model in the foot, it would be only a matter of time before it fell flat on its face. God was on the move in secular history. He had allowed (or provided for) Reformation state-churches which, in exporting themselves to the New World, would soon find themselves nothing but competing religions. He had yet to serve up the curve ball of a corporate model that would eventually make them even more cripplingly institutional than they had been. And he had still to pitch them the collapse of the corporate model in our own time. Once again, God was — and still is — throwing sinkers.

7. From Christendom to the Corporate Model

As we begin to talk about the actual demise of the Christendom model of the church, I want to put an image in your mind. When a structure is on fire, it frequently burns brightest just before it collapses. It may have periods of energetic (if possibly extinguishable) burning before that; but when the fire-feeding air at last has free access to a building, truly uncontrollable combustion takes place — and the whole structure collapses on itself in a spectacular explosion of sparks.

So it was with Christendom. The match, if you like, that lit the fire was Constantine's Edict of Toleration. The fire thus ignited soon burned brightly enough, particularly in Byzantium as it headed into the catastrophe of the Islamic conquest. Through the Middle Ages in the West, though, it died down at first for lack of a sufficiently ornate secular order to keep it going, but it revived nicely in the more elaborate culture of the fourteenth and fifteenth centuries. But with the advent of the nation-states and their newly minted churches — and above all with the invention of the divine right of kings as Christian doctrine — the high wind of the recently discovered notion of individual liberty fanned the structure of Christendom into its final flame-out. As the sixteenth century progressed into the seventeenth and eighteenth centuries, however, another and even more powerful wind came up to feed the flames. *Newness itself* — *nowness* rather than pastness, *modernity* as such — became the criterion for judging what was truly important in the life of the culture. The period of the Renaissance and afterward was a time of new states, new churches, new learning, new music, new art, new philosophy, new science, and, of course, a whole New World. The Oxford English Dictionary's first citations of the word "modern" are all from the sixteenth century. For most of the history of the human race prior to that time, what was to be cherished was the past. We had come from a golden age "back there" somewhere, and we looked longingly to it for our deepest self-definition. But now — and very quickly indeed, compared with the relaxed pace of earlier history — the bright present (and the even brighter future that would inexorably flow from it) became the touchstone of human life and institutions. The modern world had arrived: the eye at the top of the pyramid on the back of the U.S. dollar bill would look out on a *novus ordo seclorum,* a "new order of the ages."

It's hard to overestimate just how new that order felt to the thinkers of the late seventeenth and eighteenth centuries. The old order was not merely falling down; it was *to be brought down* in the name of all that was new and right. The Age of Reason had arrived, and the intellectual and societal creations of previous ages had either to submit to it or get out of the way of progress. "Darwinism" — the conviction that history is an evolutionary march onward and upward — didn't start with Darwin; he was only a convenient, if controversial, peg to hang it on. Modernity as the key to the future had long been the new intellectual toy of the Enlightenment. The divine right of kings to manage the new order — and, along with it, even the right of God to obtrude himself upon the clockwork of a now self-sufficient world — went up in smoke. The "watchmaker" God of deism replaced the intervening God of revelation. God had only a single function left: to make the world once and then get out of its way, leaving the philosophers (not the theologians) in charge of figuring out what his intentions for it may have been. After all, it was such a perfect world, a world so capable of managing its own future, that even the thought of miraculous intervention in its affairs would be an insult to its integrity. As a matter of fact, many of America's founding fathers were deists; and in a good many of the churches of the time, deism was even more popular than religion. The United States was never more modern than the day it was hatched.

But think for a moment what that meant for the Christendom model as it had been exported to the New World. True enough, since no model of anything ever puts itself out of business voluntarily, the mini-Christendoms of the Reformation era did indeed set themselves up as established religions when they first arrived. But dissenters were everywhere, and the devout took to the totally disestablished frontier — and a rather large number of the movers and shakers of the time simply called a plague on all religious compartmentalization and declared it irrelevant if not iniquitous. The net result was that when the great American experiment of a new order was finally put down in black and white, the idea of the establishment of religion by the state was summarily put to sleep.

And that, said John, was that. Fifteen hundred years of Christendom went up in a shower of sparks. If it was hard to overestimate the force of eighteenth-century philosophical newness, it's practically impossible to make too much of what the First Amendment to the Constitution did to the mini-Christendom model. The church was no longer a legitimate force for the management of state affairs, and vice versa; it became, with the stroke of a pen, marginal all over again. Old patterns die hard, of course: even now, considerable efforts are being made to act as if America is, or at least should be, a "Christian nation." But it never was one; and unless it goes back on its original charter, it never can be. The church in the United States has always been "the churches." For all practical purposes, from the Constitution to the present day, it has been little more than a clowder of sectarian cats competing over religion.

Which, according to the argument of this book at least, is a disaster: a falling back to a default position that the church should never have occupied in the first place. What had once been a *societal* religious institution was now shorn of its formal, societal role: all that was left for it (since its creative, Gospel-centered imagination had for so long been dormant) was to turn itself into a religious institution pure and simple — or, better said, into a host of such institutions. The Anglicans became the Protestant Episcopal Church of the United States of America, the Scots became the Presbyterians, the Germans, the Swedes, and the Norwegians became three different flavors of Lutheranism, and . . . you fill in the rest. But in so doing — and this is the central point of the present chapter — they all picked up from their new historical context yet another model: they became *religious corporations* in the style of the newly invented *business corporations* of the day.

Before taking up the corporate model in earnest, however, let me point out that much the same kind of thing was happening back in Europe. Take England, for a single example. From the beginning of the mini-Christendom model, it had been one of the principles of British political life that Roman Catholics could not hold office or have much part at all in public life — for the obvious reason that they were not members of the Church of England. The Roman Catholic Duke of Norfolk may have been allowed to wander at large and sit in the House of Lords, but no other Romanists were thought suitable for much of anything. By the early nineteenth century, however, that hard-and-fast rule was becoming more and more irrelevant to politics as it was actually being done. The Enlightenment had undercut its theological footings, and the libertarianism of the American and French revolutions was eating away at its timbers. Consequently, when enough members of Parliament were finally convinced of the pointlessness of continuing to exclude Roman Catholics from British politics, somebody made a motion to stop the pretense, and Parliament passed the Catholic Emancipation Act.

One other British illustration. The University of Oxford entered the nineteenth century as substantially what it had been since the Reformation: a clerical preserve of the Church of England. Edward Bouverie Pusey, a priest of the church who became Regius Professor of Hebrew in 1820 — and who, as a leader of the Tractarian (later, the High Church) Party, was one of the great backward-lookers of all time — felt utterly at home there. But by the time he died in the 1880s, Oxford was well on its way to becoming (much to Pusey's discomfort) the secular institution it now is.

None of this is to say that the church was uniformly conscious of the changes that were going on. A good deal of time and energy was spent on the project of renewing and revitalizing the collapsing mini-Christendom model by taking it back to the perceived ecclesiastical glories of various periods of the Christendom model itself. The Tractarian movement in England was just such a reversion: the hope of the church, it insisted, lay in a return to the catholic faith of the ecumenical councils of the undivided church that the Church of England had never intended to abandon. In other words, while the Tractarians disagreed with the rather "protestant" confessional twist that had been given to the Thirty-Nine Articles of Religion for some three hundred years, they remained convinced that a "catholic" confessionalism of sorts was still the right way to proclaim the church's self-identity. The same thing was true elsewhere. It was Pope Pius IX who, in 1854 and 1870, added to the already considerable confessionalism of the Roman Church since the Council of Trent by promulgating the dogmas of the Immaculate Conception and Papal Infallibility. Nor were Protestants to be outdone on the faith-as-assent-to-propositions front. Alarmed at the hostility between science and religion stirred up by the popularizers of Darwinism, they added to their own already heavy confessional burden by cultivating the biblical literalism that eventually blossomed in the Auburn Declaration and the subsequent Fundamentalism of the early twentieth century. As if the Westminster Confession, for example, hadn't been enough, they tacked onto their lists of binding propositions the entire text of the Bible, *now to be read in one sense only.*

As I see it, the taproot of all of this defensive reversion to the creedal devices of religion was the uncriticized assumption that *religion itself* was still, as before, the church's proper business. One of the giveaways to this was the general Protestant reaction to *Pio Nono's* declaration of papal infallibility. The pope, he maintained, would infallibly pronounce the mind of the church on questions of *faith and morals* whenever he spoke *ex cathedra* — that is, in his official capacity as the supreme teacher of the church (the precise definition of "official" being left somewhat vague). Protestants woke up from their religious slumbers only long enough to howl at the nerve of any one human being, however guided by God, to make such a claim in advance of the questions to be asked. But then they promptly went back to sleep and dreamed their same old dreams about *creed* and *conduct* as the heart and soul of the church's real business. They rinsed off the objectionable, imitation-vanilla coating of infallibility on the pope's medicine, as it were; but they swallowed without a thought the bitter pills of religion and moralism that still give the church bad breath. To this day, when a priest or minister eats lunch while waiting to address the Rotary Club, the program chairman in the next seat knows what the clergy are really up to even if they don't — and he gets it right in one short sentence. "I'm not much for all that doctrine stuff, Reverend, but I do know we need people like you around to keep these kids from going hog-wild over drugs and sex." He may not like Christian confessionalism (though he's willing to let parsons do "what they have to do"), but he loves Christian moralism. If the church ever seriously got over its infatuation with faith-and-morals, there'd be no more free lunches for the clergy.

But if religion came through the collapse of Christendom with hardly a scratch, the status of the church as an institution underwent major surgery. The *business-oriented* corporations of the nineteenth century on which the church would now choose to model its life were a far cry from any other institutional models it ever tried out. They weren't at all like the postexilic, Jewish *ekklēsía* of its beginnings; they were hardly like the collegial, familial, and kingly models of its first three centuries; they were certainly not like the various societal-institution forms it acquired under Christendom; and even those business corporations themselves were not like the corporate entities that had preceded them since the sixteenth century. This last point is important. For three hundred years, there had been a steady multiplication of "Trading Companies" — of commercial institutions that were able to raise capital and conduct their affairs under the law as state-created if fictitious "persons." Unlike partnerships, these companies could survive the death of any or all of their members; and unlike other associations that might so survive, their status as *government-endorsed* private enterprises made them a force to be reckoned with. The great trading companies of the Renaissance and afterward were, most of them, monopolies granted by the state *for public purposes* — for activities like exploration, dock-building, and trade — which the government wanted to see pursued, but which it deemed more convenient for private citizens to undertake. In a word, they were state-sponsored capitalism. As a matter of fact, at the start they could be created only by the king, though as the power of kings diminished, various parliaments took over the business of chartering them.

In sharp contrast to that pattern, the corporate business ventures of the nineteenth century, while they were indeed "public persons" (the state still reserved the right to create and regulate them, though it did precious little of the latter), were actually dedicated to the pursuit of *non-public* ends — that is, to business transactions as we now understand them: the gathering of *capital* to finance the production of *goods and services* that can be sold to *consumers.* And by yet another of God's breaking pitches (or was it a knuckle ball?), the church found itself at a point in its history where it was in a similar situation. The Missionary Movement of the nineteenth century was a distinctly *transactional* operation. The church had goods and services, namely, the Gospel (in theory — though it was "salvation" or the "saving of souls" in practice); it had consumers, namely, the "heathen," wherever they might be found; and it needed capital to get the operation off the ground. At first, an ad hoc system of private subscription seemed sufficient to do the trick. But as the various missionary societies of the eighteenth and nineteenth centuries extended their reach and had to grub for wherewithal, the business-corporation model of organization began to look more and more attractive.

The experience of the Episcopal Church in the United States is instructive. As the numerous (and frequently competitive) missionary agencies operating under its sponsorship began to look as if they might benefit from consolidation, the church invented a corporation that would achieve it for them. By a resolution of its General Convention, it created a corporation named "The Domestic and Foreign Missionary Society" — and, by a brilliant fiat, it declared every member of the Episcopal Church a member of that corporate personage. But as I said, such fictitious persons have a life of their own. So when the missionary enterprise abruptly and embarrassingly ran out of breath in the twentieth century, guess what the church did with The Domestic and Foreign Missionary Society? Did it abolish it? Of course not: a corporation, being far more angelic than human, can never will its own death. What the church did was convert the Society into yet another corporate entity, namely, The National Council of the Episcopal Church — which, when even that persona had trouble breathing, was yet again spared the indignity of expiration by being converted into The Executive Council of the Episcopal Church. Not only that, but beginning around the end of World War II, the Episcopal Church (along with a fair number of other mainline national churches, including the Roman Church) started down the road of changing its product line from the old "goods and services" of Overseas Mission to a succession of more trendy gizmos: in the fifties, to Education; in the sixties, to Social Justice and Civil Rights; and from then till now, to Gay Rights, Women's Rights, Liturgical Revision, Inclusive Language, and general Religious Liberalism — followed, of course, by what we presently have: Gay Wrongs, Spirituality, Traditionalism, and something that looks suspiciously like general Religious Conservatism.

It's the old, old story of modern life: if a corporation isn't doing what it's supposed to, the one thing you must never do is kill it off, or even wonder about whether you should have created it in the first place. You may change its logo or find it new widgets to market; but you must never — even after it has gone through three redefinitions and a dozen new products hand-running — question its right to go on existing. Only two things can destroy a corporate persona: revolution from the inside or catastrophe from the outside. You can't reform an angel; violence is the only solution.

But back to the "business-model" incorporation of the church in the nineteenth century. The local churches had already begun taking corporate form from the late eighteenth century on. As I

[80]

said, even in America the body politic still reserved the right to grant corporate charters. To oblige the churches, therefore, "religious corporation laws" were placed on the books in various states. But as the "product-to-consumers" model of the secular corporations became normative, the now corporate church followed suit — with a wrenching twist: *It went from selling salvation to the heathen to selling religion to its own clientele.* That this was a step onto a slippery slope should be obvious. Given the time it would take for the mid-twentieth century to arrive, "the church" (the *marketor*) would be redefined as "the clergy," and "the consumers" (the *marketees*) would go from being the "lost" out there to the "found" in the pews. The church, having once been an obligational society (however imperfectly defined), would now degenerate into a consumer-driven marketing operation dedicated to the servicing of existing accounts.

This downhill slide had relatively little effect on the national denominational churches because they were already so committed to the corporation model that they were far down the slope of corporate futility. But what it did to the local units of those churches was devastating. Under the medieval version of the Christendom model, a parish church in a given place was simply the church of all the citizens in that place, just as the church at large was the church of all the citizens of Europe. And it was "catholic," at least in one sense, because everybody available (provided you didn't count too carefully) was in it. If the local churches of the Middle Ages fell somewhat short of the best definition of catholicity, they were still such random grab-bags of high and low, rich and poor, wise and foolish that they looked like a fair approximation of universality. And for a while, the state churches of the Reformation managed to keep up that same, everybody-belongs appearance. But as the splintering of the church progressed — and, in particular, as it progressed to the New World — the pretense of catholicity became harder and harder to maintain. The churches were by then competing versions of the Christian religion: a given town could have several such churches; a given city, dozens.

However, as the nineteenth century wore on into the twentieth (and the corporate model became increasingly consumer-driven), the local churches became little more than franchises of brand-name businesses vying for market share. Membership statistics and financial viability were made the measure of every unit's success or failure. And when you add to that the tendency of American demographics to change more and more with each passing year, you get the whole passel of undesirable results in which we now find ourselves. For one thing, denominational "brand loyalty" has given way to church-shopping. Born-and-bred Methodists who move to Phoenix, for example, may try a Methodist church there; but if they take exception to the cut of the minister's jib, or the quality of the choir, or the dowdiness of their child's Sunday School teacher, they may hie themselves to the Episcopal church — until, of course, they move to Tulsa, where the search for the right religious shop begins all over again.

For another thing, the temptation to make the local franchise bigger and better becomes almost insuperable. The mega-church with four thousand members, a staff of seventy-five, and thirty-six programs turns into the ideal — into the ecclesiastical counterpart of Wal-Mart. For yet another, this "supermarket" vision is realizable only in certain circumstances. Depending on which church judicatory you're talking about, anywhere from one-third to two-thirds of its local units have already become marginal in terms of the corporate ideal. Predictably, the home offices of those "problem churches" can think of only one thing to do with them: set them a "growth goal" (read an "ultimatum of," say, two-hundred-fifty members in five years or less) and revoke the franchise if they don't come up to corporate snuff. For still another thing, all the clergy, mega or mini, who try to turn back the tide of marginality begin to burn out at an alarming rate. And for a last (though the list could go on and on), the burnout doesn't usually happen soon enough to prevent such clergy from committing actionable peccadilloes that scare the wits out of ecclesiastical bureaucrats and their ever-watchful insurance companies. The church becomes prey to product-liability suits over such things as "sexual harassment" and "exploitation"; the offending clergy are run out of their franchises; and the church (which is supposed to open its catholic arms to everyone, sinners included) ends up looking like a condemnatory piece of work that never heard of grace or Gospel. And all for the bottom-line reason of keeping a corporation from losing its angelic shirt in a lawsuit. My, my. As I said, there may well be some good intentions behind our current alarms and excursions over sexuality. But we're certainly smashing a lot of Gospel china in the process.

Indeed, far from following the secular lead and paring our corporate structures back to a leaner and less cumbersome condition ("less is more"), we are proceeding full-bore in the direction of involving additional classes of church members in the corporation's trials and tribulations. The guidelines now being produced by panicky judicatories for dealing with the "clergy misconduct" brouhaha do not stop at *clergy* misconduct. On the principle that misery must be provided with company even if the proposed company doesn't appreciate the invitation to misery, the churches are busy manufacturing computer-aimed, armor-piercing artillery programmed to fire automatically at church-school teachers, organists, choirmasters, parish secretaries, janitors, and anyone else who might get the corporation in financial Dutch by lifting so much as an eyebrow in the service of sexuality.

The sad result of this insistence on taking as much of the church as possible down with the foundering corporate model has been to endanger even further the church's catholicity. We are supposed to be witnesses to the fact that God in Christ has taken away the sins of the whole world. But by insisting on the moral irreproachability of even minor functionaries in the witnessing community, we are effectively saying that we cannot have in our midst any recognizable representatives of the sinfulness that is so obviously God's cup of tea. Which is manifest nonsense, of course, because one of the things all Christians are supposed to do ad nauseam is tell God what miserable sinners they are. Quite frankly, it makes the church look a bit like a carpenter who, while he claims to be the best woodworker in town, tells you that unfortunately he can't repair your house because he's allergic to wood.

But the mischief doesn't end there. Corporate overstructuring still continues to plague the church. The national churches are, by and large, bureaucracies that could be eliminated without a single tear shed outside their elaborate but minimally productive precincts. But even at the local level, every "successful" church operation is organized to the point of counterproductivity. A North Dakota Lutheran Pastor's Conference, for instance, can ask me to speak, rustle up my fee, and close the deal in a week; but a community mega-church in Ohio can sweat the arrangements through committee for six months and still not come up with an answer. It's Parkinson's Law all over again: *Work expands to fill the time and resources available for its completion.* And it's the Peter Principle, too: *If you do a job well at the lower levels of a corporate structure, you will be promoted over and over until you finally land a job you can't do —* and there you will sit forever as an impassable barrier to getting anything done at all. Many a true word has been spoken in jest.

One final disaster of the church's adoption of the corporate model, and we are done with this chapter. Ecumenism — the effort to heal the church's divisions so that its unity and catholicity might come back out of the shadows — has been one of the brighter ideas of twentieth-century Christianity. But the devices by which corporate-minded ecumenists have tried to bring about that happy outcome have been, on the one hand, wide of the mark, and on the other (as far as I can see), notably devoid of even the slightest divine cooperation. The God of history does not seem to me to be terribly solicitous about getting several old Lutheran horses joined at the hip to form a single new corporate beast. Nor do I think he is particularly interested in putting all his feed money into a Lutheran-Anglican Concordat that may do little more than frighten the horses and make liars out of the trainers who sign it. He appears, in fact, to have something quite different in mind.

My own theory about the twentieth-century ecumenical movement is that it doesn't need fixing because it ain't broke. Take the ecumenical successes of the so-called liturgical movement as an example. After the Reformation, each new church went its own way in matters of doctrine and liturgy — and all of them, one way or another, lost their grip on the Eucharist as the central act of the church's worship. Confessional statements of what the Holy Communion *meant* became the reasons for having it (or mostly, not having it more than once in a while) — in spite of the fact that the church had more or less faithfully stuck with it as the Sunday service for fifteen hundred years, *just because Jesus said so.* From the Reformation right up to this century, there were so many contradictory views of what the Eucharist was supposed to mean that there was simply no *theological* way of getting it back where it belonged.

But the God of left-handed intervention has more than one string to his bow. Beginning in the 1920s, in out-of-the-way places like the Abbey of Maria Lach in Austria, certain people who just happened to like studying the history of worship began to find *liturgical* rather than theological reasons for the centrality of the Eucharist. And this underground "liturgical movement" began rather quickly to spread from the Roman Church, to the Anglican Church, to the Lutheran Church — and eventually even to such habitually non-liturgical traditions as the Presbyterian and the Methodist churches. By and by, therefore, almost everybody's church had a band of liturgical terrorists inside it — a band which, contrary to all reasonable expectations, actually began to make ecumenical headway with its insistence on the centrality of the Eucharist.

And so it is that all the churches mentioned above now have not only official formularies that put the Eucharist at the center of things but also a common lectionary: the same set of Bible readings for every Sunday over a three-year cycle. Local implementation of those changes, of course, varies from place to place and church to church. But nothing was so broken about the church that the fix couldn't be put in without a scrap of corporate scheming. Think about that. This monumental and practical change came about through no corporate mergers, no negotiations between churches — and, above all, no ultimatums from one church that other churches had to do things its way or else it wouldn't play. It just happened; and when it had happened far enough and wide enough inside each church, the votes necessary to carry the legislation implementing the change were simply there for the counting.

One other illustration, this time of a corporate approach to ecumenism that I find premature, to say the least. When the

Lutheran-Anglican Concordat as now proposed comes up for ratification by the ELCA and the Episcopal Church in 1997, it will require a number of stretches on both sides. To keep the Episcopalians happy, the Lutherans will have to accept the ordination of their present bishops by bishops in apostolic succession, and they will have to promise that all future Lutheran pastors will be ordained only by such bishops. As a swap, the Episcopalians will have to promise to accept all present Lutheran pastors as possessing valid priestly orders (even though they weren't so ordained), and also to sign on the dotted line of the Augsburg Confession. In short, everybody will get his or her favorite drink, but only at the price of swallowing something else that tastes awful. I don't know about you, but I'd rather just keep dating than get married on the basis of an arrangement like that.

Especially since I can see a better way — a non-corporate, "liturgical movement" way — of getting Lutherans and Anglicans to the point at which they can play house together happily. What we do is this. We give up on trying to sell our own versions of ministry or confessional statement to each other. All our sales pitches for bishops or doctrines were dreamed up almost five hundred years ago, and we've had plenty of time to resolve them on the basis of their original terms if we could. But we haven't. So we just cash in our chips from the old, confessional-principles casino and simply keep talking to each other and visiting each other's shops until we spot a way of acing out the entire problem.

I'll even tell you what I think the ace will turn out to be. As we inch our way toward celebrating the Eucharist regularly, we will all begin to treasure more and more the notion of *priesthood:* of *the priesthood of Jesus* to begin with; of the great but largely neglected Reformation insight of *the priesthood of all believers* — that is, of the priesthood of the church itself; and finally, of *the ministerial priesthood* of those who are ordained. And when we arrive at that point — when whole bunches of Protestant ministers take great delight in thinking of themselves as priests (which is beginning to happen even as we speak) — then the job will be done without any corporate fix whatsoever. We'll simply say that because the priesthood of Jesus was already declared to be in those ministers by the sacrament of Baptism, they've been priests all along; and we'll tell them that now that they're *acting out* that priesthood ministerially, we no longer have the slightest need or desire to confer it on them. Because the truth is that we're not just trying to sell them a widget called priesthood or a program for manufacturing it; what we really want is to see it *used* in ordinary practice. Once that happens, we're all home free.

A final warning and we're ready to move on. Professor Charles Issawi of Columbia University once wrote a humorous-serious piece entitled "Issawi's Thirty-two Laws of Social Motion" in which he described how institutions change. At the end, he appended a thirty-third law of profound importance: *"On the other hand, nothing is ever the end of anything."* I've said that Christendom is dead and that the corporate model is derelict; but that doesn't mean everybody knows they are or will be content to let either of them rest in peace. In the minds of many, for example, there is still a conviction that America can rise up as a Christian society again if only we can quash all the liberal talk about "pluralism," root out "secularism," and get religion back into public life. In fact, a good deal of the steam behind the "Contract with America" is generated precisely by the prospect of the resuscitation of Christendom as such. I don't think that will work, of course; but on the off chance that it does, it will be even more devastating to the church than to the nation. It will mean a crippling return of the church to the religiosity that never should have been and never can be its real subject. But the push for it is on, and it's not going to stop now — and it probably has a longish, if not indefinite, future. So too with the corporate model of the church. It may be irrelevant, but that doesn't mean it won't continue to flourish here and there. Wherever a local church has the numbers and the money to keep it clear of the catastrophes of marginal status, lack of funds, and crumbling buildings, the angel of the institution will be able to persuade everyone involved that St. Timothy's or First Pres. not only will but deserves to go on forever just as it is.

Time now at last, therefore, for a look at where we are as we stand on the brink of the twenty-first century.

8. The Church in the Marketplace of New Models

So far this book has been something of a jeremiad against what the church has been doing with itself for the past two thousand years. While I haven't written it in high prophetic anger, I've at least worked myself up to the occasional outburst of low prophetic dudgeon — of an episcopalian sort of fury, if you will, that's more wry than savage. Still, I'm quite convinced that I'm doing the work of a prophet in the best sense of the word. Prophecy (to quote the old bromide) is not foretelling but *forthtelling*. Only dabblers try to gratify your curiosity about what's going to happen; the true prophets confront you with what is actually going on *now*, no matter how much it hurts or threatens, so you can walk into the future with your eyes open. They don't, in other words, hand you a timetable with a list of all the stops on the line; they tell you that there is a train, that the God of left-handed power is in charge of it — and that you'd be well advised to hold onto your hat.

But the best of them also do something else. To repeat what I said earlier, the prophet Jeremiah had two phases to his career. The first (before the Babylonian Captivity of the Jews actually occurred) consisted almost entirely of fulminations against the unfaithfulness of God's monumentally dense people. But after those people were actually in captivity — after the *passion* of Israel in the Exile had begun in earnest — he became a prophet of *hope and comfort*. He began, to quote his own words, with the castigation of their sins: "Therefore once more I accuse you, says the LORD, and I accuse your children's children. Cross to the coasts of Cyprus and look, send to Kedar and examine with care; see if there has ever been such a thing. Has a nation changed its gods, even though they are no gods? But my people have changed their glory for something that does not profit. Be appalled, O Heavens, at this, be shocked, be utterly desolate, says the LORD, for my people have committed two evils: they have forsaken me, the fountain of living water, and dug out cisterns for themselves, cracked cisterns that can hold no water" (Jer. 2:9-13).

But in the end he leapfrogged himself all the way into a proclamation of grace worthy of Paul: "The days are surely coming, says the LORD, when I will make a new covenant with the house of Israel and the house of Judah. It will not be like the covenant that I made with their ancestors when I took them by the hand to bring them out of the land of Egypt — a covenant that they broke, though I was their husband, says the LORD. But this is the covenant that I will make with the house of Israel after those days, says the LORD: I will put my law within them, and I will write it on their hearts; and I will be their God, and they shall be my people. No longer shall they teach one another, or say to each other, 'Know the LORD,' for they shall all know me, from the least of them to the greatest, says the LORD; for I will forgive their iniquity, and remember their sin no more" (Jer. 31:31-34).

I stand without apology, therefore, in that great tradition. If in this chapter I shall give you rather more of my ironic fury than I have up to now (though still, it will be the indignation of someone who is fonder of alcohol, tobacco, and tomfoolery than of blame), I will, like Jeremiah, end this book in hope. Because no matter what mistakes the church has made or will make in its life, it remains the divine mystery it was from the beginning: the *body of Christ*, the sacrament — the real presence in the world — of the incarnation of God in human flesh. I would dearly love to be around long enough to see the church wake up to what it really is. But in the likely event that I am not (or in the even more likely one that you give up on me before the last chapter), I shall give you the comfort of our deepest identity in two sentences right here. Despite the disasters of all our models so far, the church will always be the sacrament of the Mystery of Christ. And even if it hides that mystery under bushel after bushel of forms that do its witness no favors, it will always have the Gospel to rediscover and proclaim. The Mystery of Christ in the church is God's mystery, not ours. We may give ourselves problems with it; he has none.

On, then, with a look at the new models of the church currently on the market. Once again, *context* is everything: in the present collapse of every form we've known, the next form or forms of the church will not drop down from heaven or be given to us directly by God. Nor will it or they be dredged up by a nostalgic return to the past: no one can go back; our true home always remains resolutely in front of us. Nor above all will any helpful model of our life be cooked up by a committee: what we need is the white horse of the Apocalypse that gallops in over the ruins we have made, not some lumpy camel put together by ecclesiastical management-consultants. Instead, we shall have to settle for being what we are: a sacramental fellowship consisting entirely and only of human beings. We can think only of models that are already in the market-place of our minds. A glorious future shape of the church will be achieved only if our hands and hearts can do better than the ones that gave it its less-than-glorious past.

Therefore the question we most need to ask ourselves is not some idle query about what the next model of the church will be. Rather, it's a twofold *contextual* question: What are the new models we're already trying on; and what other models are currently lying around that we might try out? Needless to say, in answering either part of that question we shall come up with both good and bad models — and, given my slightly choleric disposition, you will not be surprised if I find more bad ones than good. It's the price of hanging out with prophets. But I'm not alone: the "next form of the church" is a hot topic right now, as well it should be: the dreadfulness of all its forms — past, present, and future — has already been stigmatized by a host of experts. Accordingly, let me first give you a shopping list of the models that I think are currently in the showrooms and then have at them to see how many turn out to be *religious, institutional,* or *uncatholic* lemons. Here's the list.

MODELS WE'RE ALREADY BUYING:

The New Corporate Model;
The Mega-Church Model;
The Professionalism-of-the-Clergy Model;
The Renewal Models, comprising the Church-Growth Movement,
the Spiritual/Charismatic Model, and the
Cursillo/Marriage-Encounter Model;
The Church-as-Advocacy-Group Model

MODELS WE HAVE YET TO CONSIDER:

The Alcoholics Anonymous Model;
The Marginal-Church Model

In the automotive jargon of the day, most of these models are "previously owned," but some still have a new-car smell about them. Let's kick some tires, slam some doors, compare the sticker prices, and test-drive everything on the lot.

The New Corporate Model (a Japanese import, though I'm told it was originally an American idea). As I've already pointed out, even secular corporations have become disenchanted with the pyramidal, top-down structure of business institutions as we've known them. The almost military, chain-of-command hierarchy of most modern corporations has ended up making either bad decisions or no decisions at all. It involves too few minds; and the minds at the top, according to the Peter Principle, are usually not the best minds. So the latest bright idea for rescuing the corporate structure has been to chuck the vertical style of organization and put in its place something more horizontal — something more like a round-table process involving everybody in the outfit. This style has been given a number of buzzword names: "shared decision-making," "employee ownership," "dinner-table rather than boardroom management," "the corporation as family rather than army," and so on. All things considered, it's not a bad idea; and the church (alert, for a change, to the drawbacks of its own corporate structure) has latched onto it with considerable enthusiasm. I would even admit that some aspects of it, particularly the *familial* ones, lie very close to what the church really is. But because it is, in the last analysis, a gambit designed to *save* corporations rather than put them out of business, I have to point out that the temptation of the church to ape the secular corporations *for that reason* is almost as insuperable as it is dangerous — and that to give into it will invariably be tragic.

Besides, there is a very large sleeper lying in the church's adoption of any seriously horizontal model of organization. The *ministry* of the church may seldom have been a thing of beauty and a joy forever, but it was always supposed to stand within the church as an authentic, even an *authoritative* voice for the proclamation of the Gospel. Shared decision-making is all well and good. But when the sharers decide, for example, that grace is for the birds, or that sinners can't be kept in the fold, or that the church is a club for those who can come up with the moral wherewithal to meet the dues, some apostolic voice is supposed to speak up and tell them all to get lost. The ordained ministry is not just a collection of Jacks and Jills who have been to seminary and, having gotten bravely over it, are now treasured for their skills as administrators, entertainers, amateur psychologists, and all-purpose handypersons. They have a duty and a right to say what is and isn't Gospel — and they have a solemn obligation to tell the church it will have to drop dead to all such anti-Gospel nonsense if it really wants to live.

I've spent the last twenty years of my theological career harping on the centrality of death and resurrection to the proclamation of the Gospel. I started down that road back in 1974, when I attended a clergy conference at which James Forbes (now the Senior Minister of Riverside Church in New York City) was the speaker. The conference was held, as I recall, at Grossinger's — though it may have been at one or the other of the *glatt kosher* pleasure domes in the Catskills that the Diocese of Long Island seemed to prefer as a venue for the edification of its priests. In any case, Jim Forbes spent three days pounding away at one point: *The church can't rise because it refuses to drop dead.* The fact that it's *dying,* he said (I'm paraphrasing him, not quoting), is of no use to it whatsoever: dying is simply the world's most uncomfortable way of remaining alive. If you are to be raised from the dead, the only thing that can make you a candidate is to go all the way into *death*. Death, not life, is God's recipe for fixing up the world. (See Jesus: "Those who save their life will lose it; those who lose their life for my sake and the Gospel will save it.")

I won't belabor the farther reaches to which I've pursued that insistence; suffice it to say that I've embodied it in every book I've written since. My point here, once again, is that while there's a great deal that's good about the "Japanese" model of corporate structure, it remains a model of something that still can't die of its own accord — and therefore is a model that the church can safely touch only with a twenty-foot pole. That we now sense the futility of the corporate model as received is all to the good. But if we rely on a new version simply to galvanize that model back to life, we're going to get burned. Because our sense of its failure has already been one of the driving forces behind many of the other irrelevant stabs we've made at resuscitating it. The corporate church on the right thinks that a "return to Christendom," or to "Christian family values," or to "law and order" is just what the doctor ordered. The church on the left imagines that the corporation will come alive if only it takes a stand against "racism" and "sexism" and for "multiculturalism." And the church in the middle doesn't know what it thinks — only that it's scared and wishes the whole war of buzzwords would go away.

But right, left, or center, the church's real need is not to save its life from the downward drift of the corporate model; it's to go with the flow all the way down into the death of that model itself. Only then can it rise. The corporate model is, hands down, the worst thing that ever happened to the church. And the angel of the corporation is the very thing now standing most in the way of our seeing that. As long as a national church judicatory, or a Methodist Conference, or a Presbyterian Session, or an Episcopal Vestry, or even the group-minded Official Board of a Michigan Mega-Church is an institution that cannot lay down its life in order to forgive what it can't condone, no version of the New Corporate Model will ever be more than a surreptitious device for teaching everyone a

Heimlich maneuver to save something so far gone it would be better off dead. Because the angel of the corporation never sleeps. It can co-opt twelve hundred people as easily as twelve: unless it's actually destroyed, nothing new will happen. Which brings us, naturally enough, to:

The Mega-Church Model (meets California emission standards, but can't stop at the edge of a cliff). Like Jeremiah speaking to Israel before the Captivity, I have not a kind word to say for it. Its sheer size makes it corporately successful in the extreme — angelic to a fare-thee-well. Its consumerism is flagrant. It sells what the market demands: religion, not Gospel; goods and services, not confrontation; life enhancement, not redeeming death. Besides, it's far too close to being the entertainment industry at prayer. It provides prime-time nursery care (complete with big-screen TV messages to summon the parents of intractable children), gymnasiums for "Christian aerobics," mini-dramas and sitcoms during services, in-house bookstores and T-shirt marts ("the church-front store"), feel-good songs with sticky lyrics and marshmallow melodies — and, above all, the consolations of soda-pop theology. In short, it's Wal-Mart from start to finish: it stocks only what sells and doesn't give shelf-room to what doesn't. But size and numbers guarantee nothing except the lowest common denominator of everything. Remember television? When there were just three networks, NBC had a symphony orchestra and CBS had Captain Kangaroo — and even then we called it a wasteland. Now we have fifty-odd channels, and *Melrose Place* is all over the place. So what do you think we're going to have when there are five hundred channels? Quality programming? Don't hold your breath. You haven't seen from wasteland yet.

But the last and saddest thing about the mega-church is the rest of the churches' rush to imitate it — and their almost universal unhappiness at not being able to. It may be the Home Shopping Network on its knees, but it's not the church. It may cater to a clientele large enough to make the mainline churches green with envy; but if you've got a good little restaurant, why should you waste your time being jealous of the fast-food chains? The mega-church isn't catholic, it's just big; it's no model for an outfit with a God who thinks small is the cat's meow — and who has regularly given flat tires to every stretch limo the church has historically tried to drive. So thank you very much, Mr. Dealer, but no thanks. Mega-church? No sale.

The Professionalism-of-the-Clergy Model (practically new, but spends a lot of time in the repair shop). This, of course, is not so much a model of the church as it is of the ministry; but it's such a lemon that it deserves a resoundingly low rating all its own. There was once a time when the ministers of the church were free to be almost anything they liked as long as they took a reasonable stab at preaching the Word of God and administering the Sacraments. Bishops dabbled in politics, priests wrote endless volumes of the-ology, and English country parsons sought renown for compiling concordances or growing the largest vegetable marrows in the county. But with the advent of the business-corporation model of the church, such liberty became a thing of the past. Thenceforth they would be employees whose roles were defined not by God or their own human interests but by the passing whims of the cor-poration. Parish administration became a required subject in the seminaries, right up there with all its adjunct activities — like counseling (in spite of the fact that a great many ministers, like a great many non-ministers, can't counsel their way out of a broom closet); money-raising (though the reason given for raising the money is usually the support of the corporate budget, not the liberation of the faithful from the religion of money); and a host of other fringe competencies such as running computers, fax ma-chines, copiers, youth programs, board meetings, Sunday schools, and parish fairs.

Moreover, because the clergy were often badly paid, they ac-tually welcomed this professionalizing of their labors and went on to form clergy associations — unions, quite frankly — in order to raise the level of their remuneration for services rendered. But since mere employees rarely have the self-esteem needed to ask for big money, they modestly pegged their salaries to those of high-school teachers and police sergeants — fellow professionals one and all, to be sure, though not anybody's idea of people making out like bandits.

But four funny things happened on the way to professional-level pay. One was that as the corporate model marginalized more and more of its units — which couldn't even fix the roof, let alone raise salaries — the number of places that could support full-time professional clergy shrank alarmingly. The second was that at the same time, the rate of ordinations in many churches skyrocketed. Everybody and his sister, practically, wanted to be a minister. So as the number of corporately viable parishes went down, the number of persons to compete for them went up — and that in turn created a buyer's market for clergy services which insured that the corporation would still be in a position to get bargain help. It was just another example of flameout before the collapse of a structure: the blaze of clergy professionalism isn't going to last much longer, but a lot of clergy are still going to get burned financially.

The third thing was that they also got burned personally — that is, *burned out* — as a result of all this pseudo-professionalism. It's often said that if either Jesus or Paul applied for the pastorate of a contemporary church, their names would be the first ones struck off the list. But in fact, *nobody* can tackle a job calling for such a lethal combination of omnicompetence and groveling without a lot of smoke and mirrors. To be masterful yet docile, authoritative yet deferential to everybody, powerful yet charming, and totally busy eighteen hours a day yet always available — this cannot be dignified as a paradox of the Gospel; it's a recipe for personal shipwreck.

Incidentally, I can say this because even though I have worked as a priest of the church for some forty-six years, I have never thought of myself as working *for* the church. As I've said in other places, I've had a *vacation* to the priesthood. What monies I was paid by the church were gravy to me. Uniformly thin gravy, admittedly; but then, if I wanted more I went and found it where I could (or couldn't, as the case might be). And there's one more thing: I have been "let go" (that's the polite word; "fired" is more like it) from every position I ever held in the church. This is true even of the job I now hold on sufferance until March of 1996.

Unless the Angel of the Vestry unaccountably dozes off, I shall retire with my record of unacceptability to the corporate church intact. On God's grading system, I shall have gotten straight A's in prophetic illegitimacy.

Be that as it may, the fourth thing that happened on the way to clergy professionalism was the ultimate irony. Because of the fear of lawsuits over sexual misbehavior, all the ministers who were so carefully trained in the arts of counseling, confidentiality, and warm personal relationships are now being told in no uncertain terms to see no one more than six times in a year, to keep the office door open and the secretary stationed in the next room, and to Refer! Refer! Refer! So much for professional status. The angel gave it as a carrot, and the angel took it away with a stick. I say, Good-bye and good riddance.

On, then, to the *Renewal Models* (nice cars, some of them, but they make lots of strange noises). Take the church-growth movement. It sounds all right when it's idling, but when you get it on the road it runs like every other attempt to jump-start the corporate model. Its tacit assumption is that every church that isn't presently coming up to corporate scratch in terms of numbers, money, or program not only can but *should* improve its performance in those respects. And therefore, when it's taken seriously, nobody can hear the still small voice that may be suggesting just the opposite for most of them — namely, dropping dead to the corporate model — if they really want to be the church. I'll say a bit more about this when I come to the marginal-church model. Here, let me simply give you a variation on what I've already said about death and resurrection. If there are any places in the church that have death staring them in the face, it's precisely the marginal units of the corporate model. Every Diocese, every Presbytery, every District Conference has a baker's dozen or two of churches that the authorities would dearly love to see dry up and go away. But the church-growth hype just encourages them to fight the very death that will be their salvation if only they'll trust God and grab it with both hands. In the name of renewal, "church growth" may be preventing the very renewal it claims it wants to see.

I know. Those are not kind words. But . . . , etc. Jeremiah . . . , etc. And all that.

Take next the spiritual-charismatic version of the renewal model. I'm not about to beat up on the Holy Spirit, but I do have a large bone to pick with some of the "spirituality" types who currently like to blame their irrelevancies on him, her, or it. Selling spirituality to modern Christians is like selling patriotism to Americans or motherhood to June Cleaver: it's so simply and unarguably "a good thing" that the mind shuts down when it hears the word. Nevertheless, my choler is such that I for one find it a questionable thing indeed. If the church is committed to proclaiming the incarnation of God in all that is human, it seems odd to me that Christians should single out something that's only one aspect of human nature and make it the be-all and end-all of the church's renewal.

To be sure, Christians may work on their spirituality — their prayer lives, their meditations, their "higher faculties" — as much as they like. But they may just as legitimately work on their tennis backhand or their expertise with an omelet pan. When we die, we lose *everything:* body, soul, spirit, the works. (I've always considered the importation into Christianity of the Greek notion of an immortal soul to be a menace to the Gospel and a theological pain in the neck.) And when we rise, we are raised up with the whole package restored in a resurrection of *the body.* God, apparently, doesn't take as dim a view of the flesh as some of us do: we're not angels, and he doesn't want us to become angels. In fact, he seems to suggest that the whole spiritual realm (see the early chapters of Hebrews) can't hold a candle to the job he did in the all-too-human death of Jesus. So I will say my prayers when and as I choose, thank you very much; but I will not kid myself that they're going to do something more for my redemption, or my status as a member of the body of Christ, than Jesus has already done for me on the cross once and for all. Spirituality is nice, but it's not necessary for salvation.

Furthermore, the very fact that any kind of spirituality now sells like hotcakes makes me suspect that the lowest-common-denominator factor is at work here as well. Between the New Age religions, the interest in psychic phenomena, and the fascination with reincarnation, there's a thriving market for a world that in the long run doesn't look much like the world we actually have. It's an escape *from* the secular that runs clean contrary to the God who came *down into* the secular. And above all, it's *religion,* not Gospel. Precisely because it's something that people can get good at quite on their own, it will produce — indeed, it already *is* producing — the very same batch of undesirable extravagances that the church has had to put up with every time it's been tried before: confusion, elitism, the uncatholic imposition of one group's standards on everybody, and the creation of a "church within the church" that you'd better join, or else. That, for the record, is also my objection to such sub-versions of spirituality as Cursillo and Marriage Encounter. It's all I intend to say about them, but I can hear my popularity rating dropping as I write.

Nevertheless, I find the charismatic version of renewal no better. It picks and chooses among the more spectacular bits of Jesus' career — the occasional healings, the odd "nature miracles," the three people raised from the dead, the two multiplications of bread, and the one water-into-wine conversion at a wedding reception — and it makes those the centerpieces of its program, along with speaking in tongues and falling down flat. It promises, in other words, to deliver *signs* when all the while Jesus quite plainly says he gives no sign except the *sign of Jonah,* that is, of death (real *dead* death) and resurrection — the first of which is no readable sign at all, and the second, a sign that can only be *believed,* not known — and certainly not re-enacted by us. Like Paul, I'm willing to let anyone who thinks charismatic phenomena are the work of the Holy Spirit say so loud and clear. But I won't sit still if they try to con the church into seeing such achievements as tests of whether it's really the church.

The last of the models we're currently test-driving is what I choose to call the *Church-as-Advocacy-Group Model.* It's being bought primarily by the upper echelons of corporate church management — by the national churches in convention assembled —

but its charms reach far down into the rank and file. Its specifications insist that the church, on any given divisive issue, must come down squarely on one side or the other. Both the right and the left delight in it. Is the question about abortion? The church must pass a resolution condemning it (or allowing it). Is the ordination of homosexuals the problem? Ditto. Is racism, or sexism, or euthanasia? Ditto, ditto, ditto — into the totally uncatholic gloom in which the church, by each vote, excommunicates approximately half its members.

What this is, of course, is *Pio Nono* all over again: the church as God's official question-answering machine spewing out definitive resolutions of every poser the world can throw at it. It is, to put it simply, confessionalism in drag — confessionalism a la mode. And we don't need it now any more than we ever did, especially since the world is no longer hanging with bated breath on our answers. The advocacy-group model is so obviously bad, and the world is so disinterested, that we ought to move as dexterously as possible to get rid of it. Every time one of these high-minded, catholicity-destroying resolutions comes up, it should be met with a carefully crafted countermotion that will permit the assembly involved to debate the question to its heart's content — and then produce a compromise which straddles the issue so perfectly that it commits the church to nothing whatsoever. Anglicans, if they haven't forgotten their stock-in-trade, might even be of some assistance in achieving that state of grace.

Time now to turn to the last of the new models on my list — the ones that no one has seriously tried yet because the first thing they will call for is the death of the corporate church. *The Alcoholics Anonymous Model* is perhaps the most immediately appealing. What I have in mind here is not the twelve-step aspect of the program but the "Twelve Traditions" that spell out the organizational and operational features of the group. These traditions set forth an entity that's astonishingly like the Jerusalem church. It has no established hierarchy, no ministerial offices, no budget, no local paid staff, no endowments, no governing boards, and no real estate. It meets in other people's buildings, uses other people's coffeepots, and gets its own members to spring for the doughnuts. There is no way for anyone to sue AA over the malfeasance of its personnel because nobody can find AA to litigate against it: it's just not a legal persona.

That sounds like the very thing we've been looking for, right? Yes indeed; but it's not likely to be bought by any corporate church, large or small. The only possible buyers would be totally defunct marginal churches (see below) who, having no status to lose, might be willing to give it a whirl. Maybe someday, though . . . and what a nice day that would be. It would see a church that doesn't condemn sinners any more than AA condemns drunks. It would see recidivist sinners welcomed back whenever they showed up instead of being given the one-strike-and-you're-out treatment currently in vogue. It would see grace and forgiveness, that's what. It would see *the church*.

Finally, therefore, the *Marginal-Church Model*. Of all the places where renewal can really begin, this is the most likely; there's just too much corporate baggage everywhere else. However, since I find that when I spoke earlier about death and resurrection I said everything I had to say in principle about the marginal church *(only a dead church can rise),* let me simply add a word here about how such a church might achieve that happy outcome in practice.

My program would be this. Whoever was in command over the dying institution at the next highest level of the corporate church — the Diocese, the Presbytery, whatever — would take the bull by the horns and kill it: close the church, dissolve its board, sequester its endowments, and sell off its property, putting the proceeds in escrow just in case the corpse ever rises and finds a use for them. Then the managers would explain to the remaining members of those churches that they were free to do anything they could think of (or nothing at all, if they so chose). A suggestion would be made, however, that they might think about holding a kind of wake on the next Sunday, perhaps in one of their homes, or in a restaurant or bowling alley that didn't open until 1:00 p.m. And if they took that suggestion . . .

Well, they might sit and stare blankly at each other to begin with. But with any luck, some free spirit (young or old) among them would break the ice with the questions they had never before been able to ask — namely: "Who are we?" "Why on earth are we here?" And, most important of all, "What do we think we'd actually *like* to do?" Having no model at all to meet the upkeep on and no known shape to whip themselves into, they would for the first time be open to looking for really new answers — honest answers — that could range anywhere from "We haven't the foggiest notion, but let's get together again next Sunday and see if anything's occurred to us in the meantime," to "We're here to be the church, I suppose — whatever that means," to "How about for openers we just try to stick with fellowship, breaking bread, and saying prayers? — maybe God will take care of the rest, if he wants any."

Those answers wouldn't sound like much of a start, of course; but then, a bunch of Galileans twiddling their thumbs in Jerusalem for nine days after the Ascension didn't seem like a grand opening, either. The operative fact is that a start can only occur after a stop. As Isaiah reminded Israel, the church's strength is to sit still: all the power, all the resources, and all the hope of the defunctly marginal lie hidden in the terrifying reality of their death. Only out of that can they live. But, having accepted that, they can model their life in any way that strikes their fancy: AA style, family style, support-group style, whatever. The only thing they need to guard against is the temptation to stop being dead, the longing to be alive and kicking again. Alive and kicking may be nice, but it's not astonishing. *Dead and kicking,* though . . . that's astonishing. That, in fact, is resurrection — and it's the only thing that can bring out the best in the church.

You're tempted, naturally, to shrug all of this off with "It'll never happen; it's just wishful thinking. Who could ever just drop dead like that?" The first answer is, you could (and you will) because you're a plain old human being who's going to end up stone cold anyway. But the second answer is that if you happen to believe that Jesus is your resurrection, you might even get a kick out of being allowed to be nothing for a change. So it's not exactly wishful thinking: in either case, death is the closest thing to a vacation you're ever going to get.

But, on the other hand, you're right: It'll never happen, at least not as long as a single shred of the angelic, corporate mentality is left. I'll even prove it to you. Your life and my life can be good, bad, or indifferent; but we can afford to relax because we know we're going to lose it all anyway. But the angels can't relax because the only thing that matters to them is that *they shouldn't die*. If you know a train is coming, you don't have to think about it: you can go get a beer, eat a sandwich, or take a nap. But if your biggest concern is that a train *shouldn't* come, then you stand on the platform and keep yourself wide awake to the danger. *The corporate church can never admit the train is coming:* it's always on the lookout for even the tiniest threat, however far down the track, to the life it doesn't dare lose. Therefore, since renewal comes only out of death, it's impossible for the corporate church to be renewed. Q.E.D.

9. *The Brighter Future*

I do owe you something more, though. However gratifying it may be to stigmatize the shortcomings of all previous (and some present) models of the church, it will not do to let it go at that. Two urgent questions now confront us. The first is this: Since our possible future forms are already lying about in the context that God has led us to by our history, *How will we be able to recognize a "good" form if we happen to meet one walking down the street?* And the second question is this: Since nothing is ever the end of anything — and especially since no previous form of the church was *all* bad — *What aspects of earlier forms must we be careful not to throw out when we give the infant church its reforming bath?*

I think the guidelines for answering those questions are already present in the argument from history I've been making throughout this book. Take first the matter of *recognition*. In order for us to be able to know a good form when we see one, we will have to keep ourselves light-years away from the un-astonishing, Gospel-obscuring mistake of thinking that we're trying to find a *religious model* for the church. Every time we meet something that looks like a religion, we must give it the widest possible berth. Any form we adopt must be such that it disposes us to shout from the housetops — both to those inside the church and to those outside it — *"By grace you are saved, through faith"* — not "Here is the perfect recipe for getting your act together."

[104]

Because the Gospel of grace is the only thing the church has that finally distinguishes its message from the "religious" droning that surrounds us. The world is by no means averse to religion. In fact, it is devoted to it with a passion. It will buy any recipe for salvation as long as that formula leaves the responsibility for cooking up salvation firmly in human hands. The world is drowning in religion. It is lying full fathom forty in the cults of spiritual growth, physical health, psychological self-improvement, and ethical probity — not to mention the religions of money, success, upward mobility, sin prevention, and cooking without animal fats. But it is scared out of its wits by any mention of the grace that takes the world home gratis. Therefore, the first test of any new form of the church must always be: Is it sufficiently *unacceptable* to the world? Is it *non-religious* enough to get the church out of its twenty-century-long love affair with religious respectability? If it isn't, we should have no truck with it.

For grace takes the agency of salvation *out of human hands,* whereas the heart's desire of every child of Adam and Eve is to keep it there — to strive endlessly to find something we can do to make ourselves *legitimate.* But grace makes all our efforts to legitimize ourselves irrelevant because it proclaims us already legitimated by the work of Someone Else, without a single effort on our part. And therefore while grace in fact makes us totally and giddily free from both the necessity of "good" works and the fear of anybody's condemnation, it has the inevitable effect of making us feel as if we ourselves have been declared *illegitimate.*

Point one, therefore: Any "new" form of the church must be one that not only keeps our *illegitimacy* squarely before our eyes but enables us actually to relish it, and to relish the uncomfortable freedom it gives us. Its first word to us — the primary thrust of what any new model leads us to think we should be up to — must be looked at long and hard. If it starts to tell us that there is something we have to do *in order to* anything whatsoever, we should bid it a firm good-bye. It must be tolerated only if it can speak to us before all else about what we *already are* — about the redeeming work that has already been done in us and for us by God in the

Mystery of the incarnation of the Word. We have no need to tune into something that will give us reruns of medieval morality plays about the "dangers" of sin, or of the Reformation's long-running series on the same subject — any more than we need more mainline-preachers' shows about "how to cope" or new mega-church extravaganzas selling "personal fulfillment." The next form of the church should enable us to realize that we are at a *party* of outrageous proportions; and it should make us want nothing so much as to shout the invitation to that party at the top of our voices.

Point two follows from that: Any form we pick must have *no built-in bias* against non-conforming behavior in general and sin in particular. That this will narrow our field of choice severely is obvious from the word "form" in non-con*form*ing. The favorite indoor sport of almost all the religious models we have heretofore adopted has been getting people to toe the line creedally, cultically, and morally. To be sure, absolute formlessness in these matters is neither desirable nor possible. The church in any given age will always be a *material,* a *sacramental* proposition. Just as, in the celebration of the Eucharist, a line must be drawn somewhere between things that bespeak a recognizable obedience to Christ and things that do not — between materials, for example, that are reasonably like bread and wine and materials that are not, like Twinkies and Coke — so too throughout the church's life. But for all that, no model of the church that dispenses entirely with creedal forms, liturgical prescriptions, and ethical standards can ever serve for an outfit that is stuck with three thousand years' worth of history and Scripture, two thousand years' worth of theological efforts to say what it does and doesn't think, and a duty, by the incarnation of God in human flesh, to have at least some normative opinions about how human beings ought and ought not to behave and to treat others.

But if the church of the future cannot be formless, neither must it be over-formed. We've taken that tack for too long. As far as our *historical consciousness* is concerned, we've cut ourselves off from our Jewish roots and invented principled anti-Semitism in the bargain. On the *theological front,* we've taken two exceedingly minimal creeds and overlaid them with vast compendiums of doctrinal shibboleths. And in the realm of *morals,* we've talked so loudly about shoulds and shouldn'ts that we've eclipsed the forgiveness of sins. In these respects, therefore, we must shop for a new model of the church that differs *only in degree,* not in kind, from the models we've bought in the past. It simply must be a vehicle that can put up with an extremely diverse group of operators and passengers but still function as authentic transportation for a church sent to deliver the Good News to everybody — not just as a parked car in which to sit and chat about who shouldn't be allowed in. Once again, given our preference for "religion," such a model will not be easy to find; but its tolerance of Sunday drivers will make it easy to like if ever we come across it.

Which brings me to point three: While the church of the future will inevitably be an *institution of sorts,* its form must be as modestly institutional as possible. The model we're looking for should not have a tendency to steer in the direction of self-preservation rather than people-preservation. That was what was wrong with both the Christendom and the corporate models. The church is supposed to be a fellowship of persons knit together by a common faith in Jesus, not an organization above and beyond persons that shackles them together by institutional rules. Scripture calls the church a body made up of many members, not a head existing all by itself or a collection of parts held together by externally applied pressure. But the Christendom model pulled badly in the direction of "aboveness" and "headship"; and the corporate model wandered in the direction of letting the market that the church was courting dictate the product the church was supposed to sell.

Accordingly, the future institution we most need will have to be an odd institution indeed: it must be able to love persons even at the price of hating itself. It will have to have a neurotic compulsion to put itself out of business if that's what it takes to keep its members on board. Frankly, I've never come across an institution like that. But if you ever meet up with such a paragon, let me know; I'd love to see it. I suspect it will look like an outdoor wedding reception that refuses to stop on account of rain. In short, it will look like the marriage of the Lamb to the New Jerusalem.

Above all, therefore, if the church of the future has to be an institution at all, it must be one that is concerned with what God is concerned about — namely, *persons.* That will be difficult in the extreme, because as I've already said, all institutions are fundamentally *angelic,* not human. But in order to provide you with a more concrete example of what any given ecclesiastical institution might have to do to put human beings before its own self-interest, let me give you a composite illustration drawn from some parish churches I've known. Just one note: keep an eye on the Capital Letters.

Once again, I give you Old First Steeple Church. To begin with, consider The Official Board. Right now it neither recognizes persons nor contains any. Its Steering Committee — the only three Functioning Agents in the Parish — makes all the decisions, subject only to rubber-stamping by The Board. (That is how The Steering Committee refers to the titular Decision Makers — not, please note, by using names like Mary, John, Helen, or Oscar.) Accordingly, the members of The Board are not actually persons but ciphers in a Process. And so if you ask them what The Board they constitute will do about x, y, or z, you will get a curious answer. They will not tell you, "*I* think . . ." or "*We* ought to. . . ." They will say, "I suppose *they* will decide we can't spend the Endowment Funds for soup-kitchen purposes." Do you see? Nameless, faceless Angels are in charge of the entire Operation.

Cure, therefore, in the future church? No more references to Entities, even if there are entities still lying about. Everyone has a name, an opinion, and a proper feistiness about both.

Next, consider The Budget and The Every Member Canvass of First Steeple. And consider them *in that order,* as is the custom of The Steering Committee. The Budget is arrived at by looking at last year's figures and, just to be safe, deciding to pad them with whatever modest increases The Steering Committee thinks the traffic will bear. Some consideration is indeed given to cutting expenditures because The Institution is already sailing far too close to the wind for comfort. But no consideration is given to *increasing* expenditure in order to implement projects the church really ought to be involved in. So when The Every Member Canvass takes place, The Members of the Parish are asked to support The Same Old Institution in the same old way — but only if they "think they can afford it," because The Board understands "how generous everyone has been" to God and Dear Old First Steeple and "how much that generosity has helped The Board keep the roof on and the doors open . . ." Et cetera.

Cure, therefore? Forget doing The Sacred Budget first. Long before any Canvass, beat everybody over the head (including The Board) — for months, if not all year, every year — with the principle of giving *in proportion to personal income,* not the principle of giving for the support of a church budget. Talk *percentages.* Give *personal figures.* Get people to compare what they're now giving (usually one percent or less) with what they might give if they moved up into the vicinity of, say, five percent. And do it all person by person, person-to-person, not by mail, phone, or Sunday Bulletin announcements. Foment a conspiracy with them. Get them to thumb their noses at the religion of money that keeps them in bondage with a pack of lies. Offer them liberation rather than trying to get them to buy brass polish for the *Titanic.* And only after that make up the budget. If the work of persuasion and conversion has been done enthusiastically and personally, the gross will be well beyond anything The Board even dreamed of.

Next, consider The Annual Fair. Except for the interpersonal friction it generates among the faithful who run it every year, it's another loser — another impersonal operation in which a nameless "they" (The Fair Committee) con a faceless mass (The Community) into shelling out support for a church it doesn't attend.

Cure? Cancel the whole thing for want of integrity (it doesn't respect persons, it just uses them), and then throw a "liberation dinner" for all the wonderful persons whose wonderfulness is no longer being threatened by The Damned Fair. Indeed, if the parish is on the road to converted giving, the cost of the meal can probably come out of the "miscellaneous" item in the budget.

But time has passed since we last visited Old First Steeple back in Chapter Five, and the former Pastor, the Reverend Al Hands, has passed too — into running a management-consulting business in Spokane. Sadly, though, First Steeple's luck at winning the Clergy-Placement Lottery has not improved. The Reverend Elizabeth ("Boots") Smathers was chosen to succeed Mr. Hands as Pastor. But in the third year of her incumbency, she began a love affair with the town Librarian, The Widow Winsome, and soon enough moved her into the Parsonage. Alas, however, routine eventually replaced Romance, and after a year and a half, she invited the Widow out of the increasingly contentious *ménage à deux* — much to the grief of Ms. Winsome. But the Widow, now not only grieving but aggrieved, decided to sue Pastor "Boots" for sexual harassment, and to include The Official Board of First Steeple and the Bishop in the suit, just for good measure.

The Board, needless to say, has been galvanzied into action by all this. As things now stand, keeping The Accused Pastor on staff will only mean that The Insurance Company will cancel First Steeple's coverage in the matter of the lawsuit. Not only that, but the Bishop, now also liable, will breathe threats at The Board. And the fearful and wonderful thing about the whole Process is that it will all be done *impersonally.* The Pastor, The Board will say, has been a Faithful Servant of First Steeple, and she is certainly Precious to The Divine; but sadly, she is "in need of help." Reluctantly but promptly, therefore, they will remand her to the tender mercies of The Great God Therapy. The Widow, equally precious, will be exalted to the status of The Victim. And The Board, confident that it has done more than all that was commanded, will consider itself a Profitable Servant. But I am tired of hitting the shift key while characterizing this Festival of Angelic Mischief. From start to finish, everybody will have nattered on about sickness instead of sin; nobody will have tried seriously to think of a prudent way to keep the Pastor on board *and* on a leash at the same time; and, above all, no one will have said a word about the biblical remedy for the whole mess, which is *forgiveness all around.*

I shall make an end. *The cure* in this last, worst case is simplicity itself: Tell the board to drop dead; tell the bishop to drop dead; tell the insurance company to drop dead; and in the glorious liberty of all their redeeming, lower-case deaths, let every last one of them be sued shirtless in honor of the only upper-case subject left: *The Gospel.*

But enough of that illustration. If the future model of the church must look not at all like a *religion* and as little as possible like an *institution,* there is still something positive we can say about it: It must be as *catholic* as we can make it. For the church's *catholicity* is its most remarkable and most paradoxical attribute. Indeed, the phrase "the *catholic* church" is an oxymoron: it delineates a body which, though it believes it has a truth for *all people,* nevertheless has a membership limited to only *some people* at any given time or place. Therefore every organizational model the church will ever adopt is both a vehicle for proclaiming the salvation of the whole world and a car up on blocks in which the church's members sit chiefly in order to congratulate themselves on their own safety.

To put it differently, the historical forms of the church are always both an opportunity and a temptation: an opportunity for the church to act out its belief that God in Christ has drawn all to himself, and a temptation to proclaim that belief by making adherence to the present form a precondition of his drawing. As I've said, catholicity is always the church's most endangered species. Accordingly, the catholic church, as the sacrament of the incarnation, will always be working against the grain of its models — always swimming against the currents set up by its forms.

For the *incarnation of the Word of God* — that is, of God himself in human flesh — is the root of the church's catholicity. And that incarnation is not simply the poking of the Second Person of the Holy and Undivided Trinity into a single human being named Jesus but that Person's abiding and irremovable presence in all people, at all times, and in all places — whether they know it or not, believe it or not, or like it or not. Because if you confine the incarnation to a single historical individual or series of events (or if you restrict its continuing "presence" in the world to a single entity called "the church"), you find you can express its catholicity only in terms of what I choose to call "tag-up" theories of salvation. You discover that you can extend the work of God in Christ to all human beings only if you can figure out some way for them to catch up with him. You resort to analogies like the old trick of "electricity" that children sometimes use in the game of tag: all those who have already "touched home" form a chain of hands extending outward from the phone pole, or whatever, so that the child who is in danger of being tagged by the evil one who is "it" can get the benefit of touching home without actually having to touch the base itself.

Enter here, therefore, the church's age-long flirtation with transactional theories of salvation — with tag-up versions of how the incarnation gets to us. Enter Baptism as the only source of the "electricity" by which people's eternal lights can be turned on. Enter subscription to the Creed of Pius the Fifth, or the Augsburg Confession, or the Heidelberg Catechism as the hookup without which darkness reigns. Enter, in short, Jesus as the Lighting Company of creation (complete with access fees, monthly bills, and the constant threat of cut-off for non-payment) instead of Jesus, like the sun, as the free Light of the world for everybody.

For the incarnation of the Word of God revealed in Jesus is not the *insertion* of a fix into creation at some point in time and place; it is the *sacramentalization,* at one point in history, of a Mystery that underlies all of history. The action of God in Christ is not that of a sewing-machine needle running a basting stitch through the world; it is the presence of *the iceberg of the incarnation* under the whole of creation. The needle touches only some points of history; the iceberg floats (nine-tenths hidden) beneath it all. Only in the iceberg illustration, therefore, can you see the "events" of revelation as truly *sacramental.* Only in it can Jesus be seen as the *upthrusting* of a Mystery hidden from the foundation of the world rather than the *insertion* of a new and discrete piece of business. And only in it can the church, as the Body of Christ, be seen as *catholic* — as just one more tip of the same old iceberg of the Word's incarnation that's already everywhere.

The upshot of all this for the next form of the church should be obvious. Just as we will never be able to find a form for the church that is not *institutional,* so (to turn that fact around) we will never find a model for our self-identity that will of itself be friendly to our true *catholicity*.

To begin with a profoundly unfriendly model, consider the Mega-Church once more. It's not catholic; it's just a big structure erected on a narrow base. Like Wal-Mart, its "margin of profitability" is tight in the extreme. Just as a twenty-five-cent-per-gallon increase in the price of gas, for example, would put Wal-Mart out of business in a month (it is utterly dependent on transportation over long distances for both supply and demand), so the Mega-Church relies on the same kind of margin. Not only that, but both of them create a supervening "community" that bankrupts the old business communities by siphoning off their clients (in the case of Wal-Mart, the mom-and-pop stores, and in the case of the Mega-Church, the mainline churches locked into suburbs or rural areas that can't provide big-time patronage). So much for the ersatz "catholicity of size" that for so long has been the church's preoccupying notion of its status as catholic. And all because we were tricked by the corporate model into servicing a clientele instead of proclaiming a free truth about everyone.

Which brings me to a somewhat more friendly model: Alcoholics Anonymous. Just as AA is a distinctly non-institutional institution, so its local units are less hostile to its implicit "catholicity" than are the present parochial units of the various churches. True enough, an AA meeting aims its outreach only at drunks (a group that constitutes not the whole of humanity but only a part). But in principle at least (if not always in practice), it embraces *all drunks,* not just the ones who happen to match its cultural or philosophical predilections. The church, on the other hand, has a message aimed at sinners (a group that comprises the whole human race), and yet it frequently acts as if only the sinless can be members in good standing. In practice, of course, since the church can't manage to exclude all sinners, it cannot maintain that pretense. So it has settled, at various times and places, for excluding other groups it deems unworthy of membership or office *on principle:* blacks, gays, women, divorced persons, people who fall outside the parameters of the nuclear family, and those guilty of some currently "fashionable" — and hence usually sexual — offense. That this is done in the name of high principle is irrelevant. Under the headship of the Lamb who takes away the sins of literally everybody, there is no higher principle than the catholicity that forbids the church to rule anybody out.

Accordingly, our next model of the church, while it will never be proof positive against such uncatholic nonsense, should be at least prone to tolerating maximum diversity of membership. The church is not an enclave of refugees *from the world;* it is the sacrament of God's presence *in the world* by the Mystery of the incarnation. It's not supposed to look as little like the world as possible but as much like the world as it can manage. Otherwise, the world (which is what the church's message is about) will never be able to recognize, in such a parochial culling of supposedly sinless humanity, anything even vaguely resembling its true face. It will just go on seeing in us the same old unforgiving face that already greets it in the mirror every morning. For the fellowship of the baptized is simply the world in all its sinfulness, dampened by the waters of forgiveness. As F. D. Maurice once observed, when you pronounce all the wonderful things you say in Baptism over some two-week-old who knows nothing, believes nothing, and has done nothing (and who, by and by, will know, believe, and do all kinds of cockeyed stuff), you in effect pronounce them over the whole wacky world. Our next model, therefore, should not automatically tempt us to deal with derelict thirty- or fifty-year-olds by welshing on the things we said over them when we first let them in.

Incidentally, when I wrote at the beginning of this chapter about "shouting from the housetops" the Good News that we are saved by grace through faith, it occurred to me that there may be yet another model that might be friendly to the catholicity of the future church. In fact, it's one that's already "in the house" — in the *secular context* that I've insisted is the only place in which God invites us to discover forms for the church. I have in mind the Internet. Admittedly, it has its drawbacks. It's a *virtual* community, not a real one: it stands at a quasi-angelic remove from the world of warm, furry bodies; and it's too *mental* to serve a church that's committed to the proclamation of God's incarnation in *all* that is human. But it does have some attractive features. For one thing, it has very few *institutional* characteristics: it's something that grew like Topsy — a kind of floating, conversational crap-game that lets anyone in its whole "universe" play, thus giving itself a good leg up on *catholicity.* For another thing, its conversations are not confined to the narrow business of *religion:* they cover literally everything under the sun. True, it may express its interests by purely verbal communications, and thus betray a gnostic tendency to overestimate what mere knowledge can accomplish. But as a model for a church whose greatest treasure is words about the Word — for verbal Good News *to* the world rather than strong-arm power *over* the world — it's not bad at all.

Two things about it give me pause, however. One is that the control freaks have already got it in their sights and are just itching to institutionalize the freedom out of it. I'm not so much worried about the government's putting an arm on it. (There are simply too many opportunities for fun, games, and mischief on the Net for that to work.) What concerns me more is that bickering among users over what should and shouldn't be allowed on it will result in a spate of self-imposed rules that will make it indistinguishable from any other institution, virtual or real.

The other is that I can't for the life of me see how the church can do much with it in actual practice. It might take to proclaiming the Word on the Net — thus forcing itself to be a lot more astonishing than it now has to be with captive audiences in the mainline churches or audiences captive to hype in the Mega-Church. And it certainly could make good use of the "support-group" possibilities that already exist on the Net. But Baptism on the Net? Celebrating the Eucharist on the Net? Receiving Communion on the Net? I think not. Not even TV on Sunday mornings claims to be able to bring *that* off. The church just has too much of a stake in the incarnation to allow itself to sit still for such a divorce from flesh-and-blood participation.

On balance, therefore, the Internet is not quite the model I first thought it was. But if you see something I don't, let me know.

▼   ▼   ▼

Finally, though, the second of the two questions with which I began this chapter: *Since no previous form of the church was all* bad, what aspects of earlier forms ought we at least try to make room for in our next model?

Once again let me confine myself to just two examples: the early Jerusalem church and the Christendom model. As to the first, I think I have only one thing to add to what I've already said. While the Jerusalem church model has been in the dustbin of history for so long that none of us has any cultural connection with it except for the New Testament, it remains a good criterion of what we're looking for. It was non-religious and non-institutional to a fare-thee-well; and when it responded (however reluctantly) to Paul's insistence that the Gentiles be admitted on the basis of no test except faith, it was about as catholic as the church ever became in practice. It still stands as the Lexus of church models: even if it's so expensive we think we can't afford it, maybe our admiration for its specs will at least keep us from buying a used Yugo.

On the other hand, there's the Christendom model. We've all had — and are still having — a profound experience of it. Despite its steering problems from the Reformation onward (if not earlier) and its demise as scrap in the nineteenth and twentieth centuries, it has so shaped Western civilization that it is in the very air we breathe and water we drink. And despite all the mischief wrought in its name, its benefits are blessings still. It has provided us — from Augustine, through Aquinas, through the Renaissance, through the birth of science, through the invention of political liberty and in-dividual rights, and right up to the present day — with the intel-lectual and ethical milieu in which we exist. The questions it raised are still our questions, and its best answers to them are still our answers. More than that, the Christendom model has been a store-house of images and archetypes without which our culture would be unintelligible to us. Chartres, Saint Paul's Cathedral, even the old New York Custom House all spring from it and speak of it. Byrd, Bach, Mozart, and Jazz are all its heirs; Shakespeare, Kant,

Auden, and Umberto Eco, all participants in its long conversation. And the very idea of a universe run by law, which is the incarnational foundation of our best science and politics, is its undying legacy.

And it was precisely Christendom's incarnation of the *Incarnation* itself that made it all possible. It was its firm grip on the truth that matter *matters* to God that has led us, in our finest moments, to love matter (and to love the crowning glory of matter, *persons*) as much as we do. Therefore, while there can be no going back to the days of Innocent the Third or Henry the Eighth, or to the Oxford of E. B. Pusey — or, more to the point here, to Trollope's or T. S. Eliot's fond embrace of Christendom as the framework for contemporary society — there still must be no going forward without Christendom's thoroughgoing earthiness, its uncompromising incarnationality. The next form of the church must be positively hostile to the ethereal, the transcendent — yes, even the spiritual enthusiasms that now surround us. Christendom, while it flirted dangerously with the "otherworld" of religion and spirituality, never lost its footing in this world. It didn't despise the world; it romanced it. And it didn't despise even the ignorance and brokenness of the world: it built universities for the one and hospitals for the other. For all its sometime barbarities, it did teach us to *care*. Any future form of the church that does less than that — that threatens to make us a club dedicated to our own uplift rather than a cheering section for the whole created world — should be nipped in the bud. We don't need it, and God doesn't want it. He has better things in mind for us than keeping our hearts closed and our hands clean.

Time at last, therefore, for the comfort of *astonishment*.

Epilogue:
The Astonished Heart

The title of this book may have struck you from the start as an odd one for an expedition through the often dismal swamp of church history. Let me end, therefore, by giving you the text that lies behind my insistence on astonishment as the key to renewal.

The Wisdom of Joshua the Son of Sirach (the book commonly called *Ecclesiasticus*) appears in the Apocrypha of the Old Testament. Like much of the "wisdom literature" of the Jewish Scriptures, it's a tissue of rather worldly musings shot through with a transfiguring sense of the intimacy of God to every scrap of the secular. Here is the quote that inspired me (Ecclesiasticus 43:17-18, KJV): "As birds flying he scattereth the snow, and the falling down thereof is as the lighting of grasshoppers. The eye marvelleth at the beauty of the whiteness thereof, and *the heart is astonished* at the raining of it."

That someone could look out in the very dead of winter and see in it a captivating gorgeousness has always seemed to me a perfect paradigm of the lifting of the heart I feel at the Gospel's wild proclamation of life out of death. Throughout Jesus' ministry (from the time he was twelve, no less, all the way to his resurrection), it was precisely his ability to astonish that led people to respond to him the way they did. Indeed, the Greek word *existánai* (which is the verb "to be astonished" in the passage from Ecclesiasticus I've quoted) appears no less than eight times in the Gospels (translated as "astonished"/"amazed"/"marveled") as a description of their reaction to Jesus — and it can be found six times in Acts to describe their reaction to the Apostles. But most of the preaching I hear in the contemporary church is so bereft of that kind of astonishment — so shriveled down to platitudes about life enhancement and moral uplift, so vapidly "spiritual," so un-earthy, so unlike the Jesus whose words leap like grasshoppers and devour like fire — that it's too tame to raise even a single hair. So much so, that every time I get a chance to expound Jesus' parables as the astounding, almost autobiographical depictions of the bizarre work of God in Christ that they actually are, the congregation mostly smiles indulgently and thinks it's me, and not God, who's crazy.

One note on the "physiology" of biblical images for human faculties and we're ready for the wrap-up. In our modern, Western way of looking at ourselves, we locate the intellect in the head and the emotions in the heart; but the ancient Jews had a different schema. For them, it was the heart with which they thought — remember "the thoughts and intents of the heart"? And it was the *kidneys,* of all things, with which they felt — "my heart and my *reins* trouble me in the night season." ("Reins" is from the Latin *renes,* as in *ren*ologist, a kidney specialist.) Both they and we, however, happen to agree that a human being — and God himself, for that matter — feels the most important sentiment of all with the *intestines:* they had "bowels of compassion," and we have "gut reactions" when we respond to the things that call for our deepest involvement. Be that as it may, the "heart's astonishment" works out in Hebrew to be the *mind's* astonishment. But since that puts *us* in the advantageous position of being able to hear both the fascination of the intellect and the power of the emotions in the phrase, I find it the very thing we need to fill the bill of renewal.

On with it, then. If the heart of Jesus Ben Sirach could be astonished at the raining of the snow which the *Holy Wisdom —* the *Sancta Sapientia,* the *Hagia Sophia,* the eternally creating *Saint Sophie* — has brought into being, how much more astonished should be our hearts, which now look on that same Wisdom who became incarnate for our salvation in Jesus and who now orders the world mightily and sweetly by the resurrection of the dead.

We are in a war between dullness and astonishment. Not between conservative and liberal, not between peasant and intellectual — and, above all, *not between believer and non-believer.* The modern world is dying to believe. We surreptitiously read *The National Enquirer* in the checkout line precisely because we are itching to believe even the most unbelievable stuff, if only we can convince ourselves it's astonishing. We will believe in the transmigration of souls, or regression to past lives, or the New Age religions of spiritual uplift because we find those oddities more interesting than the predictable faith-and-morals pap we persist in handing out instead of the paradoxes of the Gospel. And, as I said, we will buy any gnostic product on the shelves of those religions of right thinking just because we find in them a promise of the conquest of death which, even though it is patently false, astonishes us more than the church's tiresome recitation of recipes for personal success and its dreary preoccupation with who does what to whom in the bedroom.

Indeed, it may well be that this thirst for astonishment is the real reason for the current glut of people seeking ordination in the Protestant churches. It certainly isn't jobs: anyone in his or her right mind can see that the number of positions open is shrinking and the pay for occupying them (except in situations of corporate flameout) on the decline. What I think lies behind the stampede of candidates for the ministry to seminary is the hope that there at least they might get a handle on the incredible goodness of the Good News that the church has buried six feet deep under a pile of unalarming piffle. They may just have caught onto the profoundly biblical truth that if the general loveliness of human life as promised by preachers could have been achieved by good advice, it would have busted out all over twenty minutes after Moses got down from Mount Sinai. But it never did, and it never will: only the strange work — the *opus alienum,* the work of God's *left hand* in the death and resurrection of the incarnate Lord — can ever bring it off. It may well be true, unfortunately, that the seminarians will find that astonishing news just as dried up and withered away in seminary as they did in the church. And sadly, it may be even more true that they themselves have bought into the prevailing model of the pastor as professional Christian — of the clergy as the only "real" Christians — to the exclusion of the rest of the witnessing community. But that's beside the point: it's the thirst for astonishment that drives them. And it's that thirst that we most need to recover. Blessed are those, and only those, who hunger and thirst.

It won't be easy, though. Astonishment is a highly perishable commodity. It may be the igniting fuse of every romance, every marriage, every career, and every intellectual delight; but given the soggy march of time and circumstance, it's hard to keep it lit. In previous chapters I've held up the AA model as a possible paradigm of the post-corporate church. But after a mere sixty years now, that model itself (not so much in its "Twelve Traditions" but in its acceptance of the death-and-resurrection experience implicit in its "Twelve Steps") is in deep trouble. An article in a March 1995 issue of *The New Yorker* reported that the astonishingly radical insistence of the original movement on "descending into hell" (my phrase) as an instrument of salvation (on service to others who have hit bottom as the key to your own sobriety) is being eroded by the preference of the latest generation of drinkers for personal "therapy" over raising the dead. Old-timers point out that service is now harder to come by: a lot of current members steer clear of someone who comes to a meeting drunk; even the number of people willing to make coffee is down. In this, AA is an *admonitory* model for the emerging church: no new form we adopt will protect us from the loss of astonishment we will suffer if we forget the Good News that *only the dead* hear the voice of the Son of God — and that only the dead, therefore, *live*. What is happening to AA, in fact, is almost a perfect parallel to what happened to the original Jerusalem church. It, too, started out with nothing but the proclamation of death and resurrection, but in sixty years it was up to its chin in the distractions of religion. The subtitle of the piece in *The New Yorker* put it in a nutshell: "Now that America believes less in help-your-fellow than in blame-the-person-who-made-you-a-victim, can Alcoholics Anonymous [read "the church"] still get its message across?"

But I promised you comfort, so here it is. The Lover who restores the world in Christ is not the God of the philosophers or even the theologians (unless they are very astonishing theologians indeed). And that God is certainly not the god of the inner-harmony-through-self-help gurus. The God incarnate in Jesus is an utterly *desirable* God. He (or she) runs the world from beginning to end by the radically astonishing device of *romancing* it into being out of nothing. It leaps into existence in a fit of longing for the incarnate gorgeousness that calls it; and it leaps out of its death by the drawing of that same gorgeousness and the voice of that same calling. Creation is a *dance of desire.* In the long run, it hardly matters that creation's notion of what it desires is almost invariably cockeyed. The desiring and desireable God is still in charge. And when every last particle of creation — including you, me, the lamppost, and the church — ends up dead, gone, and at absolute zero, its heart will still leap up at the voice of the Beloved.

Because the church is not a club; it is a divine Mystery — the body of him who fills all in all and who, when he is lifted up, draws all to himself. We are in a dance of desire over which we have no final power to throw a wet blanket. The thirst of the astonished heart lies at the root of all thirsts, however trivial, and it is the *thirsty,* therefore — and the hungry, the last, the lost, the least, the little, and the dead — who are the sacraments of the church's hope. Only fools, of course, willingly embrace those conditions. But the divine Fool who died and rose needs only one of them — himself — to bring the dance to its wild conclusion. Even if all the rest of us are tripping over our own feet to the end of time — even if we spend every one of our days trying to wallflower our way through the corporate church, the mega-church, the Christendom church, the country-club church, or the self-improvement church — even if we never get the dance of desire right, God never gets it wrong.

Resurrection reigns wherever there is death; and with it comes the joy of the really Good News: the dance into the New Creation in Christ will always be alive and well. *Desire,* however we manage it, can always explode into astonishment.